PAPER ACTION TOYS

E. Richard Churchill

Illustrated by James Michaels

Sterling Publishing Co., Inc. New York

For Dillon Andrew Churchill, a young man with real talent

Library of Congress Cataloging-in-Publication Data

Churchill, E. Richard (Elmer Richard)
    Paper action toys / by E. Richard Churchill ; illustrated by James Michaels.
        p.   cm.
    Includes index.
    ISBN 0-8069-0368-6
    1. Paper toy making—Juvenile literature. [1. Paper toy making. 2. Toy
making. 3. Handicraft.] I. Michaels, James, ill. II. Title.
TT174.5.P3C475   1993
745.592—dc20   93-23860
                                                                    CIP
                                                                    AC

10 9 8 7 6 5 4 3 2 1

First paperback edition published in 1994 by
Sterling Publishing Company, Inc.
387 Park Avenue South, New York, N.Y. 10016
© 1993 by E. Richard Churchill
Distributed in Canada by Sterling Publishing
% Canadian Manda Group, P.O. Box 920, Station U
Toronto, Ontario, Canada M8Z 5P9
Distributed in Great Britain and Europe by Cassell PLC
Villiers House, 41/47 Strand, London WC2N 5JE, England
Distributed in Australia by Capricorn Link (Australia) Pty Ltd.
P.O. Box 6651, Baulkham Hills, Business Centre, NSW 2153, Australia
Manufactured in the United States of America
All rights reserved

Sterling ISBN 0-8069-0368-6 Trade
              0-8069-0369-4 Paper

Contents

Introduction

Every paper action toy in this book moves. Sometimes the wind causes the toy to move; at other times you'll supply the energy to make your paper toy move.

These paper action toys aren't difficult to construct. A few require a bit of careful folding, but if you just follow the written instructions and look carefully at the illustrations, you won't have any problems. Some projects can be constructed in just a few minutes; others take a bit longer. All of them may be used over and over.

The materials needed to make these toys are things you have around the house. There's nothing that you have to buy, unless you need a new roll of tape or a tube of glue.

Start saving some construction materials which you'll need for paper action toys. Cardboard tubes of all sizes will be used for several of the toys. These tubes include the enormous ones which come inside rolls of gift-wrapping paper, as well as smaller tubes from rolls of bathroom tissue. An empty round hot-cereal carton will come in handy, as well.

Save empty cereal boxes and other cartons which are made of the same sort of material as cereal boxes. A few old file folders will also be useful.

Have a special storage place for the construction materials you save. A cardboard box in the corner of your room would be perfect. Don't leave empty cereal boxes and cardboard tubes lying here and there about the house.

You'll be using a pair of sharp scissors, cellophane tape or masking tape, and a bit of paste or glue. From time to time you'll need a few straight pins and several paper clips. A few feet of string will be needed from time to time.

A ruler and a pencil are necessary for some projects. When you need to score lines, a ballpoint pen and a dull table knife will come in handy.

From time to time you'll want to color or decorate a project. Crayons, felt-tip markers, or paints will do the job nicely.

When you need to make circles, a compass is good to have, but round dishes or the ends of food cans will work just as well.

1
Action Fun and Games

The paper action toys in this section are all games of one sort or another. All of them may be played by just one player or used as contests with two or more players. The first three action games are so easy to play, you'll understand them instantly. However, they take a bit of practice before you'll get really good at them.

The final two games in the chapter require some mental work. They are action puzzles in which you'll be moving a few game pieces from one place to another until you've mastered the puzzle. You'll have great fun challenging others to solve the puzzle you've created.

Action Flipper

Making an *Action Flipper* takes about a minute. You'll spend hours playing with it as you improve your accuracy.

Cut out a strip of cereal-box material 8″ long and 2″ wide. Fold one end along the dotted line shown in Illus. 1. This fold is ½″ from the end of the flipper. Crease this fold so that the end stands straight up from the rest of the flipper.

Illus. 1

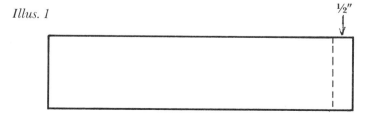

½″

Illus. 2

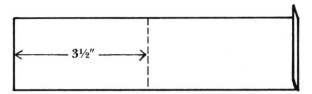

Bend the flipper along the dotted line shown in Illus. 2 so that the 3½″ end is under the rest of the flipper. Don't fold and crease the material, bend it! By bending the material, you'll create a flipper which will send a paper wad quite a distance.

Wad up a bit of notebook paper or newspaper (about 4″ square) into a tight little ball. If it comes undone, use a bit of tape to hold the wadded paper together.

Illus. 3 shows how to launch the paper wad with your flipper. Use a finger or two on one hand to hold the bottom of the flipper securely to the tabletop or the floor. With the other hand, push the flipper's top down and hold the paper wad in place.

Paper missile wad

Illus. 3

To launch the paper wad, just let go, and the flipper will do the rest. Just remember to hold the bottom of the flipper firmly in place with your other hand.

Set up a target into which you'll fire the paper wad. Actually, you'll want to make half a dozen or so paper wads; you won't have to keep retrieving one wad over and over.

Your target can be a large bowl, a pan, or an empty flat box. If you use a bowl, make sure it's fairly deep and has straight sides. A shallow bowl or one with sloping sides won't work because the paper wad will hit and bounce out.

Take turns firing paper-wad missiles at the target, and score a point for each one that hits the target.

If you wish, set up several target bowls or boxes of different sizes. Score a point for hitting a large one and two or three points for landing in a smaller target.

For variety, you can fire your missiles at small standing targets. Empty rolls from bathroom tissue make great targets. Score a point for a hit and two points if you knock over the roll.

There's no limit as to what you can use as targets. However, here's a note of caution. Always pick up all the paper-wad missiles you shoot. Leaving bits of paper lying about is messy.

When your flipper loses its spring, take thirty seconds or so and make a new flipper. You can experiment with flippers which are wider or longer than your first one. Longer flippers have more leverage and will fling the wads a greater distance. Wider ones may be a bit more powerful.

Cone and Ring Catch

Variations of this action toy come from all over the world. It's been around for hundreds of years and has entertained millions of children.

The first step in making this paper action toy is to make the cone. Simply roll a sheet of notebook paper or computer paper into a cone that's smaller at one end than it is at the other. In Illus. 4 you see the finished cone, which is held together with a little strip of tape.

Illus. 4

Tape

The ring is even easier to make. Just cut 1½″ from the end of a large paper tube. The big tubes from the center of gift-wrapping paper rolls are perfect for this project.

When cutting rings from paper tubes, be careful. You don't want to mash the tube, and you don't want to punch a hole in your finger with the scissors.

Carefully push the end of the scissors through the side of the tube. It helps to put a roll of newspaper inside the tube. This gives your scissors something to push against and it makes certain that you don't get a finger in the way.

Have you seen the rest of my paper?

Once you've cut the cardboard ring from the tube, you'll need a piece of string or thread 3' long. Tie one end of the string around the tube, as shown in Illus. 5.

Illus. 5

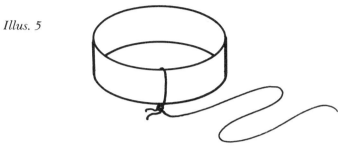

Secure the other end of the string to the cone with a strip of tape. Illus. 6 shows how.

Illus. 6

Hold the cone with one hand, as shown in Illus. 7. Toss the ring into the air with the other hand. The object of the game is to catch the ring on the cone. Then try to catch the ring twice in a row, then three times, and so on.

Once you've gotten the hang of catching the ring on the cone, it's time to play the game one-handed. Give the cone a flip as you hold it and the ring flies into the air to the end of the string. If you miss, flip the cone again. If you capture the ring, just flip the cone and the ring sails off for you to catch again.

This is a great game of skill, which you can play alone or play with others as a contest. Each player might take ten turns, scoring one point for each successful capture of the

Illus. 7

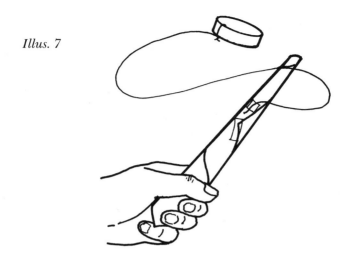

ring. Or, each player may play with his or her own cone and ring and go for a record of consecutive catches.

Ten-Tube Bowling Action

To make the bowling tubes that will be your targets, you'll need ten tubes (or more or less if you wish) from bathroom-tissue rolls. Or, use the cores from paper-towel or fabric-softener rolls and cut them in half.

If you have to cut the tubes in half, be very careful. Remember to push a roll of newspapers into the tube as you learned in the previous project. Then press the point of your scissors through the tube and into the newspapers. This will keep you from smashing the tube or poking a finger.

If you don't have enough tubes handy, you can always make tubes by just rolling a piece of stiff paper or file-folder cardboard into a hollow cylinder.

You'll notice that hollow tubes are easy to tip over. This means that you'll need to put some weight into the bottom of each tube in order for the tube to become a good pin for your bowling game.

To put weight into the bottom end of a tube, first close the tube's end. Place one end of the tube on a sheet of paper, and draw around that end with a pencil. When you remove the tube, you'll have a nice circle, such as the one shown in Illus. 8.

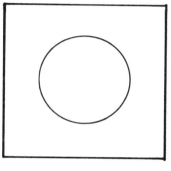

Illus. 8

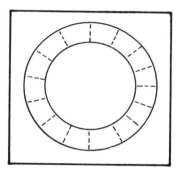

Illus. 9

Now draw a second circle around the first one. Make this circle about ½″ or so larger than the first one. Since this circle is ½″ larger all the way around, it's actually 1″ farther across than the first circle. You can use a compass or the bottom of a food can to draw this circle, or just draw it freehand; it doesn't need to be perfect.

Illus. 9 shows both circles in place. Also shown are a number of dotted lines between the two circles.

First, cut out the larger circle. Now, carefully cut in from the outer edge until your scissors reach the inside circle. That's the circle you first drew. Make these scissor cuts about every ½″ (or a bit less) all the way around the circle. Be sure you cut in only as far as the inside circle.

Now stand the tube on top of the paper you've been cutting. It looks like the drawing shown in Illus. 10.

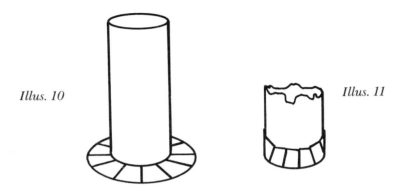

Illus. 10   *Illus. 11*

Bend each of the small sections of paper up so they fit tight around the end of the tube, as shown in Illus. 11.

You can use paste, glue, or tape to fasten these little paper tabs onto the side of the tube. If you use tape, don't pull off a long chunk of tape and try to wrap it all the way around the tube in one effort. It's much easier to pull off short strips of tape and fasten two or three paper tabs at a time onto the tube.

Once you've glued or taped all the tabs into place, your tube has one end entirely closed. Now place something fairly heavy in that end of the tube to give it enough weight to make the tube into a good bowling pin. A dozen small rocks or pebbles should do the job nicely. Dirt or sand isn't a very good idea because if something causes the paper to tear, you'll get dirt or sand all over the house.

Wad up a small piece of newspaper and push it into the open end of the tube and down onto the weights. This forms a top seal and keeps the weight in the bottom of the tube even when the tube gets knocked over. Experiment to see just how much newspaper you need to make a nice, firm wad to fill the tube exactly. If you try to press in too large a wad of newspaper, you'll tear the tube.

As soon as you've weighted all your tubes, it's time to play.

Set up your pins in regular bowling order, or in a line. You don't have to use ten pins; use more or less if you wish. Illus. 12 shows two ways to arrange the pins.

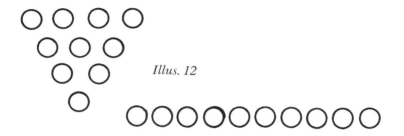

Illus. 12

Use any small ball you have to bowl with. A tennis ball will work fine, but so will an old golf ball, or a small rubber ball. Each player may have two rolls, as in bowling, or you can alternate turns until all the pins are down (if you decide to line up the pins in a row instead of a triangular formation).

For variety, color one pin red. Instead of one point, the red pin is worth two points to the player who knocks it down. Paint, felt-tip marker, or crayon will work fine to color the pins.

Another variation is to number each pin. You might have five with number one, three with number two, one with three, and one with five. Each pin knocked down scores as many points as its number.

This is a good game to make and play when you have to entertain younger children. It's fun to come back to time and time again.

Mental Action

This toy is called *Mental Action* because you have to put your mind to work in order to win. *Mental Action* takes less than a minute to learn to play, but it's harder than it looks to win when you do play.

Begin by drawing a playing board on a sheet of paper or a piece of file folder, or even a piece of cereal-box material. Each square should be 1½″ on a side. You'll need to begin by drawing a square that is 7½″ on all sides. Then fill in the inside lines every 1½″.

If your material is large enough make the squares two inches across, draw the outside square so it's 10″ on each side. The larger squares make it easier to move your playing pieces. Illus. 13 shows the finished playing board.

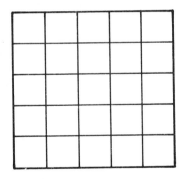

Illus. 13

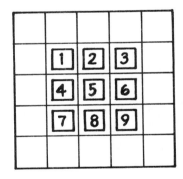

Illus. 14

Now cut nine playing pieces out of cereal-box material or from an old file folder. You can use paper for the pieces, but paper is so light, a little breeze will disturb them and ruin your game.

Make each playing piece 1″ square. Number the pieces from one to nine. Once this is done, you'll be ready to test your wits.

Set up the playing pieces on the board so that things look like Illus. 14.

Here's how the game goes. Pick up any playing piece you wish and jump it over a piece next to it so that you land in an empty square. Remove the piece you jumped over.

You may jump vertically, horizontally, or diagonally. Each time you jump a piece, you must land in an empty square. You can only jump one piece at a time.

If you decided to have piece 5 jump piece 6 for your first move, the playing board would look like Illus. 15 when the move is finished. As you can see, there are now only eight pieces left on the board.

Illus. 15

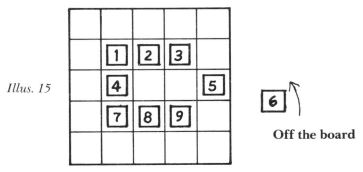

Off the board

Keep jumping one piece over another piece and removing the jumped playing piece. To win the game, you need to end up with just one piece on the playing board. Since you remove one playing piece with each jump, this means that you'll need only eight jumps to win the game.

Anytime you can take eight jumps and end up with one piece on the board, you're a winner. If you finish your final jump so that the last playing piece is in the center square then you're a *Super Winner*!

It doesn't matter which numbered playing piece you finish with. But you need to end with just *one* piece in order to win the game.

This is a great game to play by yourself or with someone else. Try to end up with fewer pieces than the other player after each of you has played one game. Use the game as a challenge to other players, once you've learned a successful combination.

Further on in the book you'll discover one series of moves which ends up in a *Super Win*, but don't look now. It's lots more fun to conquer this super game on your own.

Five-Cube Fun

The first thing you're going to learn when making this paper action toy is how to turn a flat piece of material into a perfect cube. Then you'll discover how to make five cubes, which are *Five-Cube Fun*. Sometimes players end up calling this game *Five-Cube Frustration!*

First of all, a cube is a solid figure with six sides. All six sides form perfect squares. In other words, some of the building blocks you played with as a young child were cubes.

You can make cubes out of notebook paper and they'll work just fine. If you have a piece of paper that's just a bit stiffer than notebook paper, that's better still. Some of the stiff advertising sheets that appear in magazines are excellent, if you won't mind having all the print and color on your finished cubes.

Make your first practice cube from notebook paper or typing paper. You can decide after making the cube whether you want your game cubes to be of stiffer material.

Let's make the first cube 2″ on each side, just because it's easy to fold and assemble a cube this large. Later, you can make smaller game cubes, if you wish. For your practice cube, you need a piece of material at least 8½″ by 7″ in size. If you happen to have some squared paper handy, that will make your job easier.

Measure very carefully as you draw your cube outline. Each side must be exactly like all the other sides. Begin by drawing a rectangle that's 8″ long and 2″ wide, just like the one shown in Illus. 16. Press down firmly on your pencil or

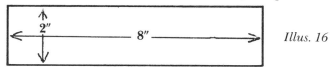

Illus. 16

ballpoint pen. Don't press down hard enough to break the pencil lead, but do make a nice, deep line as you draw. This little groove in the material will make it easy to fold along the lines in just a minute.

Lighten up on that pen, will you?

Making such a groove is called *scoring*, by the way. If you decide later to use stiffer material, such as that cut from a file folder, it helps to score the fold lines with a dull table knife. Hold the knife near the tip and draw it along the edge of your ruler along the lines you draw. That little groove will make all the difference when it comes to folding a straight line.

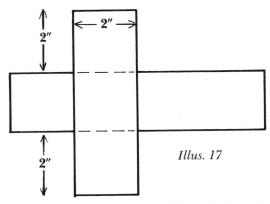

Illus. 17

Now add the crosspiece shown in Illus. 17. It is 2″ wide and 6″ from end to end. What you're really doing is just adding a pair of two by two cubes to the rectangle you drew first. Check the measurements shown in Illus. 17 before you add this crosspiece.

Add the flaps shown in Illus. 18. These flaps, which are labelled either "A" or "B" in the illustration, should be about ½″ wide. Later, if you make smaller cubes, these flaps can be just a little narrower than ½″, if you wish.

Measure and draw in the fold line that separates the long section to the right of the cube into two smaller cubes, and you're ready to begin construction.

Don't worry about all the "A" and "B" flaps and the A + squares right now; they will be explained later. Just concentrate on drawing an outline exactly like the one shown in Illus. 18.

The dotted lines shown in the illustration indicate folds you'll be making. When you first drew your cube, you drew these lines as solid lines and scored them.

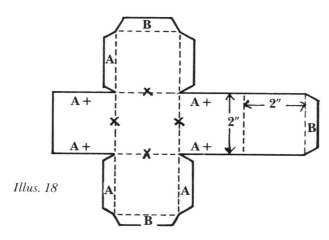

Illus. 18

Compare your cube outline with Illus. 18. If it is exactly like the drawing, cut out your cube. Once you've carefully cut out your cube, it's time to do some folding to turn your flat paper into a three-dimensional cube.

Begin by folding the four flaps labelled "A" so that they stand up. Fold each flap upwards along the scored line you drew and crease the fold. These flaps now stand up like those shown in Illus. 19.

Check Illus. 18 again. There are four dotted fold lines, each marked with an "X." Fold along each line marked with an "X" so that the square beside the fold stands straight up in the air. This means you'll have three sides of the cube with one square each standing straight up. The fourth side (the one on the right in the drawing) has two squares in it. Illus. 20 shows how things look at this point.

Once you've made these four folds and creased the fold lines, flatten the material back as it was before you made the

"X" line folds. This means that the four "A" flaps are still standing straight up, as shown in Illus. 19.

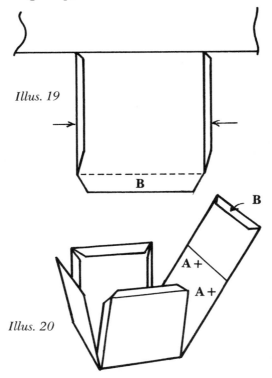

Illus. 19

Illus. 20

Now it's time to spread a little line of glue or paste along the back of each of the four "A" flaps. The back of the flap is the side of each flap that was facing down until you just folded the flap. The arrows shown in Illus. 19 point to the side you're going to glue. Don't put too much glue onto the flaps; you don't want glue running down your cube.

If you get confused at all while making the cube, just slow down and go back a step and keep looking at the drawing and comparing it to what the text says. After you fold just one cube, you'll discover that the process is really quite simple.

With glue or paste on the backs of the four "A" flaps, it's time to refold the cube along the fold lines marked with "X." Fold up the two sides with the glued "A" flaps so that these sides stand straight up.

Now fold up the other single square. It's the one on the left in the drawing. Fold it up so that it fits over the "A" flaps. When you do this, you'll see that each "A" flap fits against this square at the point it's labelled "A + ." You're now at Illus. 21.

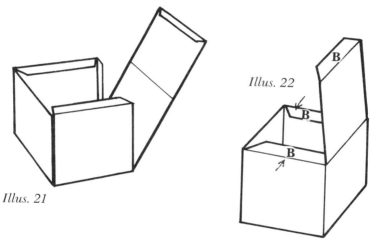

Illus. 22

Illus. 21

Press the two "A" flaps firmly against the square you just folded into place. Make certain the edges meet exactly so you have the beginnings of a perfect cube.

Now fold the remaining side up so that the final two "A" flaps fit inside the material where it's labelled "A + ." Since this side of the material is two squares in length, you'll have one square of material sticking up in the air, as can be seen in Illus. 22.

Press the glued "A" flaps firmly against the sides marked "A +" and make certain the edges match exactly. At this point you've formed a perfect little box with the lid still open. You've also formed five sides of your cube.

Now spread a bit of glue on the three "B" flaps. The arrows shown in Illus. 22 indicate which sides of the "B" flaps you need to glue.

Once the flaps are glued, close the cube by folding the final side into place. Make sure all the "B" flaps are tucked inside. Hold the top down or put a little weight on it until the glue dries. Your finished cube should look like the one shown in Illus. 23.

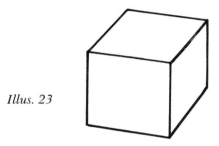

Illus. 23

If you decide to use tape rather than glue when you make your cube, tape each of the four "A" flaps into place as you fold the cube together. However, it's just about impossible to tape the "B" flaps, since there isn't any way to reach inside the cube once the top is folded down. Therefore, you'll need to place the final tape along the outside edge of the top to hold it in place.

By now you've already realized that you can make a set of building blocks if you have the time and patience. Make them a few at a time and add to the set when you have the time and energy.

Back to your *Five Cube* action toy. You'll need to construct five cubes all the same size. You can make them as small as 1″ on a side or as large as the one you just made. Take your time and be sure all six sides are square.

Once the five cubes are constructed, mark the six sides of each cube with from one to five dots, just like the dots on dice. Each cube is going to be marked differently, so pay close attention to these directions.

First of all, make your dots like this: 1 = • , 2 = •• , 3 = •• , 4 = •• , and 5 = ••• . Felt-tip markers are perfect for dotting your cubes but pencil, pen, or crayons work just fine. Be careful not to poke a hole through the material when you dot your cube.

Begin with any of the five cubes you just made. Place one dot on the top of the cube. Then turn over the cube and place three dots on the bottom. Once this is done, place the cube on the table facing you with the one-dot side back on top. Set the cube so one side is facing you. It should look like Illus. 24 now.

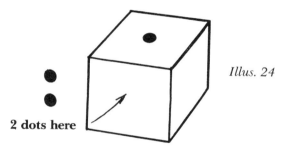

2 dots here

Illus. 24

Draw two dots on the side, or face, of the cube that's directly in front of you. Turn the cube a quarter of a turn so that the two dots are now on your left. You've turned the cube *clockwise*.

Place two dots on the side facing you. Turn the cube another quarter of a turn. These two dots are now on your left, and the first side with two dots is at the back of the cube. Check just to make sure things are going properly.

Mark two dots on the face of the cube towards you. Rotate it another quarter of a turn and draw three dots on the final face. You've now finished marking your first cube. Now it's time for the rest of the cubes.

Put five dots on the top of the next cube. Then mark four dots on the bottom.

Draw four dots on the side nearest you. Rotate a quarter of a turn so these four dots are on your left. Now draw three dots on the next side. Rotate and draw one dot. Rotate the cube for a final time and put two dots on the final side.

For the third cube, color in five dots on top and three dots on the bottom. Mark the face nearest you with one dot. Rotate the cube a quarter-turn and draw on four dots. Rotate it again and mark four dots on the next side. Finally, put one dot on the last remaining side.

Cube four gets one dot on top and four on the bottom. The first face needs five dots. Rotate and put one dot on the second side. Rotate and draw on three dots. Make a final quarter-turn and put five dots on the final face.

The last cube needs two dots on top and two on the bottom. The first side gets three dots. Now rotate the cube and draw in five dots. Rotate and draw five dots on the next face. The last side of the cube needs four dots.

After all this cutting, folding, and dotting, it's time to play with your newest paper action toy.

This is a puzzle. The object is to stack the five cubes on top of each other, so that when you look at any of the four sides of the stack you'll see one dot, two dots, three dots, four dots, and five dots. In other words, you'll have sides numbered from one to five on all sides of your stack of cubes.

The dots don't have to be in order. In fact, it's impossible to have all four sides with the dots in order from one to five. In Illus. 25 you can see two possible arrangements, each of which contains sides numbered from one to five. As you can see, the dots are not in 1, 2, 3, 4, 5 order. However, each side shown does contain five cube sides showing all five numbers.

You may get lucky and hit a winning combination quickly.

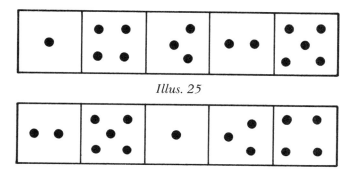

Illus. 25

If so, mix the blocks and try it again. Better still, try to find another winning combination. Just be absolutely certain you have your blocks stacked in such a way that all four sides have the numbers from one to five.

If you don't solve the puzzle fairly quickly, don't give up. Stop and look carefully at your cubes and try to decide whether you can arrive at a winning stack by turning just one cube or perhaps by changing two cubes.

As you play with these cubes, you'll begin to figure out some strategies. For instance, you know you need to have five dots showing on each of the four finished sides. Why not begin by setting up the cubes so you have five dots on all sides. Then work from that point, making little changes as you go.

Once you've solved the puzzle, it's time to challenge others with it. A good way to do this is to display the puzzle already solved. Let someone look at it only long enough to be sure the numbers from one through five show on all sides of the stack. Then scramble the cubes. Just to put a little pressure on the person you've challenged, tell him or her that you're keeping track of the time it takes to finish the puzzle.

Further on in the book one solution is included, just in case you get really stuck with *Five Cube Fun.*

2
Flying Action Toys

The five paper action toys in this section have one thing in common; they're all flying toys of one sort or another. Two are definitely outdoor flying toys. The others can be flown indoors, or outdoors on calm days.

Once you've made the *Cardboard Flying Discs* according to the designs suggested in the book, you'll probably want to design some *Flying Discs* of your own with different shapes. The same is true for the *Glider*. After making a *Glider* like the one described in this chapter, you'll have some ideas of your own.

That's the best part of making paper toys. Once you've seen how to make a particular toy, you can design one with your own ideas.

Cardboard Flying Disc

Flying Discs are positively outdoor toys, because they can sail for quite a distance. Also, they are heavy enough and fly fast enough to do real damage to things inside the house.

Begin with a piece of cereal-box material 8″ or 9″ on each side. Any similar sort of lightweight cardboard will work perfectly.

Draw a circle about 8″ across. If you don't have a compass, just draw around a plate or a pan lid that's about 8″ in diameter.

Now draw a second circle (inside the first) that's 1½″ or so smaller than the first circle. A saucer, or the top of a bowl, or the bottom of a food container will work just as well as a compass does to draw a circle.

Illus. 26 shows how things look at this point.

Illus. 26

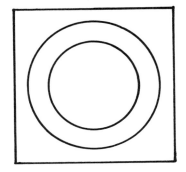

Place a pad of newspapers under the piece of material and carefully poke a hole in the middle of the inside circle. Slip the point of your scissors into the hole and very carefully snip your way to the edge of the smaller circle. Take your time and cut out the inside circle.

Once you've cut out the inner circle, cut around the outer circle. This leaves you with a hollow ring about 8″ in diameter.

Use the disc you've just cut out as a pattern and cut out two more just like the first. If you have to cut out a disc with one of the cereal box's folds running along one side of the disc, don't worry about the little fold; we'll take care of that shortly.

When the three discs are cut out, glue them into one disc that's three layers thick. Don't use so much glue or paste that it oozes out when you press the layers together, but do use enough to get a good seal. If you have one disc with a fold along a side put it in between the others. If you have folds in two, or even three discs, just make sure the fold in one disc is over the solid part of another disc, and go on with your gluing.

The instructions say not to use too much glue.

Put a book or other weight on top of the three-layer *Flying Disc* and let the glue dry.

When the glue is dry, take the finished *Flying Disc* outside. Launch it by placing your thumb on top of the disc with the rest of your hand under it. Illus. 27 shows how. Give the disc a backhand flick of your wrist, and it will take off into the air.

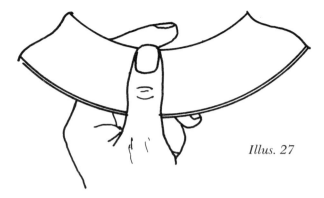

Illus. 27

After you've experimented with sailing your disc for a few minutes, you'll find it behaves differently when launched into the breeze or with the wind.

When you've made a number of flights for distance and control, try this. Bend up one edge of the *Flying Disc* along the dotted line shown in Illus. 28.

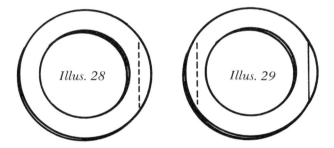

Illus. 28   *Illus. 29*

See how this changes your flight pattern.

Then bend up the other side of the disc along the dotted line shown in Illus. 29. Make another few flights.

Try the disc with the bent edges facing up and with them facing down. You'll discover the *Flying Disc* sails differently in each case. One way it's easy to control and comes in for a vertical landing. The other way it loses a lot of its control.

Finally, check out the disc with one edge bent up and the other bent down. This configuration should give you a well-controlled flight.

Now that you're an expert on *Flying Discs*, it's time to make a new design. This time you'll need three pieces of cereal-box material about 8″ wide and 12″ long.

Locate four dots on one piece of material, as shown in Illus. 30. These dots will guide you when you draw the curved sides of your disc.

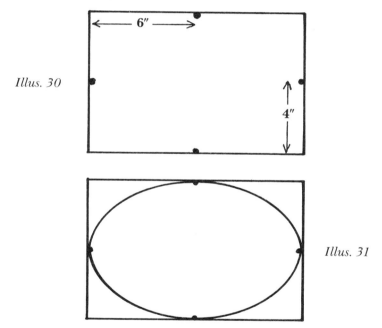

Illus. 30

Illus. 31

As you can see, the dots at the left and right are 4″ from the top and the same distance from the bottom of the material. The top and bottom dots are located 6″ from either end of the material.

Using these dots as a guide, connect them with curved lines so that you have a disc outline that looks like Illus. 31. It looks a lot like a football! Don't worry if your curves aren't exactly perfect. Just try to make all four curves nearly alike.

Now draw the inside of your *Flying Disc* so you have a disc about 2″ wide. It helps if you measure in 2″ from each of the original dots, as shown in Illus. 32.

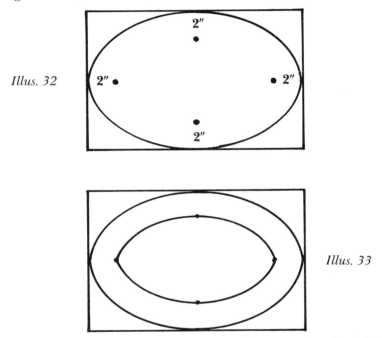

Illus. 32

Illus. 33

Connect the dots, and your new disc is shown in Illus. 33.

Cut out this disc and make two more, just as you did before. Glue the three layers together and let them dry.

This *Flying Disc* sails a bit differently from the first one, as you'll discover. Once you've flown it enough to see how it behaves, try bending the ends up or down, just as you did with the circle.

Once you've mastered these *Flying Discs* why not design one of your own with a different shape?

Eight-Piece Flying Disc

This little *Flying Disc* is definitely an indoor toy. You'll see why once you've assembled it. It just isn't heavy enough to stand up to outdoor breezes, although you might want to try it outside on a totally calm day.

Notebook paper or computer paper will work perfectly for this toy. You'll need eight squares of paper, all exactly the same size. If you make these squares 5″ on each side, you can cut two from a standard sheet of paper. This means that you need four sheets of notebook paper or other paper.

From time to time, you need a square sheet of paper and all you have are rectangular sheets. Here's a quick way to turn a rectangle of paper into a square without having to stop and measure.

Fold a lower corner of the paper over, so that your rectangular sheet looks like Illus. 34, and then cut off the shaded part. When you unfold your paper, you're left with a piece that is perfectly square.

Now back to your *Eight-Piece Flying Disc*. Take one of your eight squares of paper and fold it in half along the dotted line shown in Illus. 35.

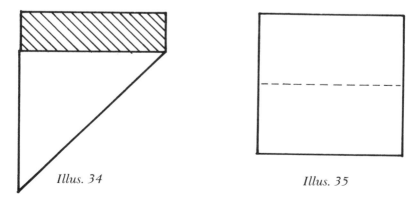

Illus. 34   *Illus. 35*

Once it's folded, it should look like Illus. 36. The dotted line in that drawing indicates your next fold. Fold down both layers at the upper left-hand corner so you arrive at the drawing shown in Illus. 37.

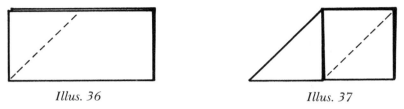

Illus. 36   Illus. 37

As you can see from the dotted line shown in Illus. 37, you're going to fold up the lower right-hand corner. Once this is done, crease both the folds you just made, and check Illus. 38 to make certain your folded piece of paper looks just like the one shown there.

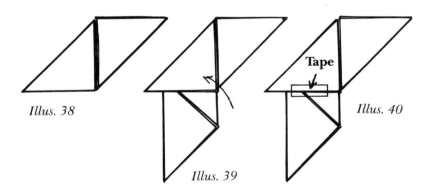

Illus. 38   Tape   Illus. 40

Illus. 39

Set this folded piece aside and fold the other seven squares of paper in exactly the same manner. Make certain that when you fold the paper in half, you always end up with the fold at the bottom of the material. This is very important!

Once all eight pieces look like the one shown in Illus. 38,

it's time to begin assembling your flying disc. Study the drawing shown in Illus. 39.

You're going to slip one folded section into the triangular little pocket formed by another of the folded sections. When you do this, be sure to slip the point of folded paper under *both* of the single thicknesses of paper that are at the top of the triangular pocket. The arrow in Illus. 39 points to these two single thicknesses of paper.

Once you've pushed one section firmly into the other, things should look like Illus. 40.

Use a strip of tape about 1″ long to fasten the two pieces together, as shown in Illus. 40.

Now work your way around the disc by inserting the folded end of one section into the little pocket formed by the section that's already part of the project. After making certain the two sections fit together correctly, use a piece of tape to hold them firmly in place.

When you get to the eighth and final section of your disc, slip it into place and tape it just as you did the ones before it. This time, however, you'll need to combine this piece with the starting piece of folded paper. Just slip the point of the first piece under the two single sheets of paper on the eighth piece. Tape this last section together, just as you did the ones before, and your disc is almost ready to test-fly.

In fact, you might give it a few experimental tosses right now. Launch it backhanded just as you did the *Cardboard Flying Disc*. However, this *Eight-Piece Disc* is better suited to flying indoors than outdoors.

After you've tested it a time or two, you'll need to do a bit of folding.

Turn over the disc so that it looks like the one shown in

You can see the eight little dotted lines in the drawing. Fold up each tip of paper along the dotted lines. Make sure

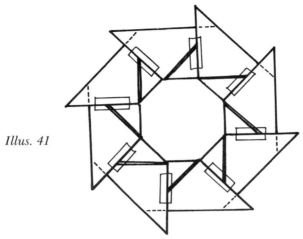

Illus. 41

these tips of paper stand straight up when you've folded them.

Turn over the disc so that the folded points are under the disc. Launch it with a gentle backhand. Your new flying disc should act like a proper flying disc by flying a fairly level flight path and coming in for a gentle landing.

You can make future discs larger than this one. You can also use stiffer material to make them strong enough for outdoor flying.

Parachute Launcher

Here's where a couple of those large gift-wrap paper cores can be turned into an outdoor paper action toy. You need two gift-wrap tubes that are fairly large; one should have a larger diameter than the other. One tube needs to be large enough so you can reach your hand and arm into it easily. The second tube should be able to fit inside the first tube. The closer the two tubes are in size, the better.

Begin by cutting off the larger tube so it's about 2′ long. Remember to put a pad of newspapers inside the tube when you push the end of your scissors through the side of the tube.

Now cut off a 4" section of the small tube. Be careful.

Stop! That's not the way to do it!

Next poke two holes opposite each other halfway down from the end of this 4" section of tube. Don't poke your finger and don't smash the tube. Illus. 42 shows the piece of cardboard tube with the holes in place.

Now seal one end of the short piece of tube. A piece of notebook paper will do the job nicely. Draw around one end of the tube on the paper just as you did back on page 13. Then draw a second circle ½" or so larger than the first. Cut out the larger circle and make a series of scissor cuts every ½" or so from the outer edge to the inner circle. If you've forgotten how to do this, just look back to page 14 and see how to seal the end of a tube.

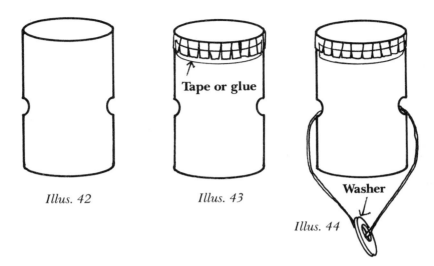

Illus. 42   *Illus. 43*   **Washer**

Illus. 44

Once you've finished gluing or taping the seal into place, the short piece of tube should look like Illus. 43.

Next, cut a piece of strong string about 3' long. Push one end through the two holes you just cut in the short piece of tube. If you have a washer or a small nut handy, push one end of the string through it and then tie the two ends of the string together. Illus. 44 shows how things look at this point.

If you don't have a nut or a washer to hang on the end of the string, it's all right. The purpose for the washer is to act as a weight on the end of the string, causing the string to hang down, so it will be easier for you to get hold of in a few minutes. Without the weight, the string still hangs down, but it's sometimes hard to get a grip on it.

Now you need four regular rubber bands, not super large ones. Form the four rubber bands into a chain. Do this by pushing the end of one rubber band through another band and then pulling the end of the rubber band back through its other end. Illus. 45 shows how to do this in case you haven't done it before.

Once you've formed your chain of rubber bands, slip a paper clip onto each end of the chain, and then push one paper clip through the same holes you just went through with the string. When you've threaded the rubber band chain through both holes in the small piece of tube your project should look like Illus. 46.

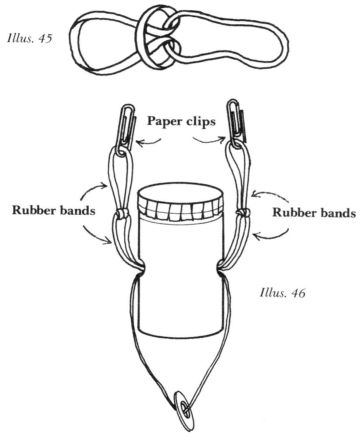

Illus. 45

Paper clips

Rubber bands   **Rubber bands**

Illus. 46

Next, slip both paper clips onto opposite sides of the long paper tube. Once the paper clips are in place, let the small piece of tubing slip down into the larger tube. Make certain the closed end of the small tube faces upward, towards the rubber bands.

Now wrap a strip of tape around the outside of the long tube so that the tape covers the paper clips. This keeps them from flying off when you launch the parachute. With the paper clips taped in place, the top of the long tube looks like the drawing shown in Illus. 47.

You've now finished constructing your parachute launcher. The string is hanging down inside the long tube. The small nut or washer provides just enough weight so that the string hangs down where you can easily reach into the end of the tube and get hold of the string.

To form a parachute, you'll need a square of cloth or plastic material about 9″ or 10″ across. A piece of lightweight plastic cut from the side of a grocery bag makes a great

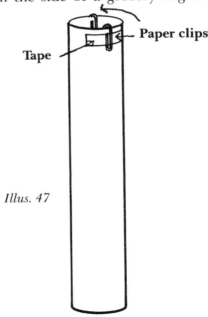

Paper clips

Tape

Illus. 47

parachute. If it happens to get stuck in a tree or on a roof, it won't matter, because you can always make another parachute in about a minute.

Cut four pieces of string, each 9″ or 10″ long. Tie one end of each string to the corner of the square of plastic, so that your parachute looks like the one shown in Illus. 48.

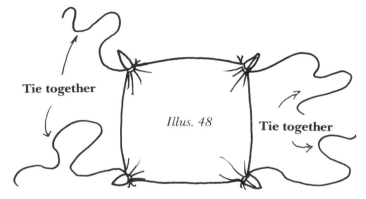

Tie together

Illus. 48

Tie together

Now tie together the two strings at the right of the parachute. These two strings are indicated by the arrows shown in Illus. 48. Do the same with the two strings on the left side of the parachute.

A larger nut or metal washer should be just about the right amount of weight to cause your parachute to open without pulling it too fast towards the earth to open. Slip the nut or washer onto one pair of strings. Wrap the string once around the washer by running the end of the string through it a second time.

Now tie the ends of the two sets of string together. Work the nut or washer down so it hangs exactly in the center of the parachute. Illus. 49 shows the weight positioned properly.

Test your parachute by holding it up at arm's length and dropping it. The parachute should open and drift to earth.

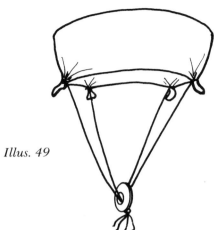

Illus. 49

If it falls too rapidly, there's too much weight for the size of the parachute. It's better to find a lighter weight than make a larger parachute, at least for this first parachute. You don't want a parachute so large that it gets stuck inside the launching tube.

Now that the parachute is assembled, it's time to take your launcher outside and test it. Don't try it indoors; this is strictly an outdoor toy.

Wad the parachute together so that the nut or washer is under the chute. Place it inside the launching tube. Check to be sure the parachute fits *loosely* inside the launcher. When you pull the inside tube downwards in a few seconds, the parachute must be able to slide down the launching tube on top of the small tube.

To launch your parachute, hold the long tube firmly in one hand. Point the end upwards at a steep angle. With the other hand get a hold on the string that hangs down inside the launching tube. Pull down on the string. This will cause the short tube inside the larger launcher to slip downwards. The parachute that's resting on top of the small tube also slips down the larger launching tube.

As you pull, the rubber bands will stretch. When the bottom of the little tube is almost at the bottom of the launching tube, let go of the string.

Illus. 50 shows the parachute launcher ready for action.

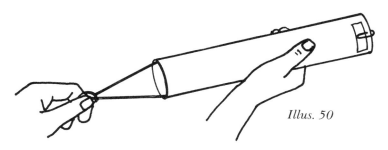

Illus. 50

When you release the string, the rubber bands snap the short piece of tube upward. This sends the parachute sailing out the end of the launcher and into the air. If all goes well, your parachute will fly upwards and then open to drift back to the ground.

Depending upon the type of rubber bands you use, you may find that your launcher needs only three rubber bands, or perhaps it may need as many as five. You can make these changes, if necessary, after a few parachute launches. If the top edge of the launcher starts to bend in, it means that your rubber bands are too strong for the launcher to handle.

If the parachute sticks in the launcher and sort of flops out the end it's probably because the parachute is too big for the tube, or you might need to wad the chute a bit tighter.

You may find you can use a larger parachute than the one you just made. Try a larger piece of material and see.

Try multiple parachutes in the tube. You should be able to launch two or three at one shot.

Remember, this is an outdoor toy. If the wind catches a parachute and causes it to drift into a tree or out in traffic, don't bother rescuing your parachute; just make a new one. After all, a piece of plastic is cheap, and it certainly isn't worth risking a fall or an accident for it.

Action Glider

Flying toys are always fun. Here's a paper action toy that you can use indoors or outdoors. It's quick and easy to make, and it should be good for many successful flights. Since it's made of cereal-box material and a piece of file folder, it's pretty tough, and it can stand up to some fairly hard flights.

You'll need two pieces of cereal-box material that are 8″ long and about 4″ wide. Your first step is to draw an outline of the glider's body, or fuselage.

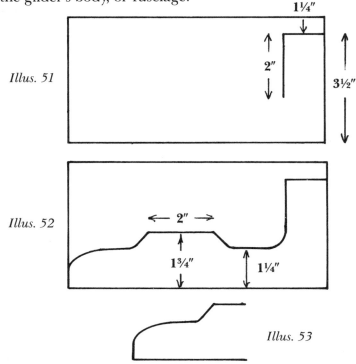

Illus. 51

Illus. 52

Illus. 53

Start at the tail section since this part is pretty much just straight lines and easy to draw. Begin by drawing a line 1¼" long that's 3½" from the bottom of the material. Then draw a line straight down from the end of the 1¼" line. This vertical line should be exactly 2" long.

Check Illus. 51 to see that your lines match those shown in the drawing.

Now draw the rest of the top of the fuselage so that your outline looks pretty much like the one shown in Illus. 52. You don't have to draw your outline exactly like the one shown in the illustration, but try to come fairly close. For instance, measure up from the bottom 1¾" to locate the top of the cockpit. Make the cockpit itself about 2" long from front to back.

Be sure that the narrow part of your glider's body is 1¼" thick, as shown in Illus. 52.

Once you've completed your outline, cut out the fuselage and tail section you've just drawn, and then use this piece as a pattern and draw another exactly like it. It's tempting to try to cut out two pieces at once to save having to draw and cut a second time. Keep in mind that cereal-box material is fairly heavy. If you try to cut two layers at once, you're likely to encounter difficulties.

If your scissors are really sharp, and you have faith in yourself, then fold your cereal-box material in half, so that the fold becomes the bottom of the fuselage. This will save you from having to tape the bottom later on. Do this only if you're certain you can cut two layers of material at once.

Your next step is to trace around the front 3½" of your fuselage on cereal-box material. This means you're making an outline of the glider from its nose almost to the rear of the cockpit. Illus. 53 shows what this outline looks like.

Make two of these drawings on cereal-box material. Cut

out both of them. You'll cut from the bottom line right up to the top line on the right-hand side of the outline, although there isn't a line there when you trace around the fuselage. Set these pieces aside for the moment.

Now for a bit of taping. Masking tape works better than cellophane tape, but you can use either kind. Place the two fuselage and tail-section pieces one on top of the other. Begin by running a couple of long strips of tape along the

It's easier to cut them one at a time.

bottom edges so that the two halves of the fuselage are now joined at the bottom. If you're really steady, you can do this with one long strip of tape. However, it's easier to hold things together and use shorter strips of tape. Of course, if you folded the material in half and cut both sides at once, you won't have to do this bit of taping.

Illus. 54 shows the bottom already taped.

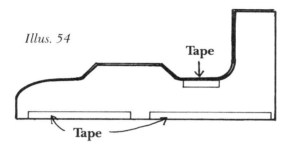

Illus. 54

Tape

Tape

Now cut off a strip of tape 2″ long and use it to tape the top of the fuselage between the rear of the cockpit and the tail section. This tape is also shown in Illus. 54.

Next, slip the two pieces shaped like the front of the glider between the two sides of the glider. Just slide them into the front of the glider so that their front ends match the nose tip of the glider. Use a strip or two of tape to hold the glider's nose together. This also keeps the two inside pieces of material in place. Check Illus. 55 to see how things look at this stage of construction.

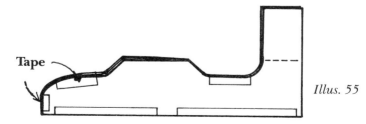

Tape

Illus. 55

The two strips of material, which are now out of sight inside the glider, serve two important functions. First, they give the glider's nose added weight necessary for it to glide evenly. Second, they make the nose a lot stronger, so it won't bend over if it sails into something hard, like a wall or a tree.

With the nose weighted let's attend to the tail section. Note the dotted line on the tail section shown in Illus. 55. Fold the top layer of material towards you, along this dotted line. Make certain this fold is parallel with the bottom of the glider. If this fold runs uphill or downhill, it will affect the way your glider behaves in flight.

Once you've folded the top layer towards you, fold the bottom layer of material away from you. Make certain you fold both layers exactly the same distance from the bottom of the fuselage.

Now tape the rear of the glider, as shown in Illus. 56. Just wrap a short strip of tape around the rear of the aircraft.

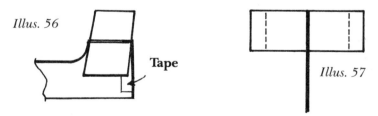

Illus. 56

Tape

Illus. 57

Illus. 57 shows a top view of the tail section. The two dotted fold lines are each ¾″ from the ends of the tail. Fold each tail tip straight up along the dotted lines shown. These upright tips form stabilizers which help keep your glider on a straight flight path.

Now make wings for your glider. For this you need a piece of file-folder material 5″ by 8″. The wings need to be stiff, but of lighter weight material than the fuselage material. File-folder material is perfect for the wings.

Fold the piece of file folder in half, so that it looks like the drawing shown in Illus. 58.

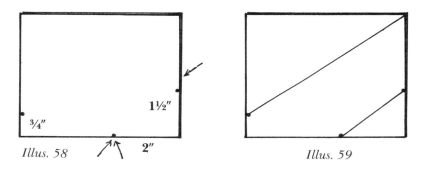

Illus. 58 2"

Illus. 59

Measure up from the fold ¾″ and draw the dot shown at the left side of Illus. 58. Then measure up 1½″ from the fold and make the dot indicated by the single arrow shown at the right side of Illus. 58.

Finally, measure along the fold from the right-hand side of the material, and place a dot 2″ from the right of the material. This dot is indicated by the double arrows shown in Illus. 58.

Now draw a line that connects the dot at the left of the material with the upper right-hand corner of the folded piece of file folder. This line is shown in Illus. 59.

Connect the two dots at the right of the material with another line; this line is also shown in Illus. 59.

Now for some cutting. Be sure to hold the folder material firmly so that the bottom layer doesn't slip when you cut. Cut along the two lines you just drew. When you've made this pair of cuts, your glider wing (which is still folded) looks like the one shown in Illus. 60.

The dotted line in Illus. 60 shows where to fold the wing. Fold the top layer of material towards you along the dotted line. Make sure this fold is parallel with the bottom fold, so that your finished glider wing will be perfect.

Now fold the lower layer of material away from you along the dotted line.

Slip the bottom of the fuselage into the wing fold as shown in Illus. 61. The front of the wing should be 1¾" from the tip of the nose.

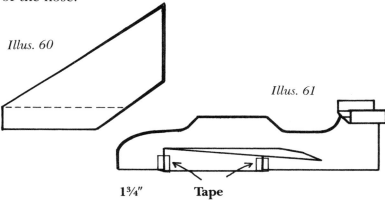

Illus. 60

Illus. 61

1¾"   **Tape**

Make certain that the fuselage bottom is firmly pushed into the fold in the wing, and then tape the wing in place both at the front and the back. This tape is shown in Illus. 61. The tape at the front of the wing wraps around and extends up the other side, naturally. Otherwise, your wing would flop around during flight.

Finally tape the tops of the wings tightly against the fuselage with two small strips of tape. You can see these pieces of tape in Illus. 62; this drawing shows a top view of your finished glider.

To launch your glider, hold the bottom of the fuselage between your thumb and your middle finger. Place the tip of your index finger at the back of the fuselage. Launch the glider with a quick, firm snap of your wrist. The glider should reward you with a nice gliding flight.

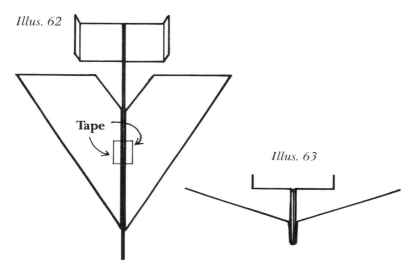

Illus. 62

Tape

Illus. 63

Make certain the ends of the tail section are straight up to stabilize the glider's flight. You'll probably discover that your glider flies best when the wings slope upwards from the fuselage to the tips. You can adjust this angle with the little pieces of tape you used to attach the tops of the wings to the fuselage. To adjust the wing height, carefully peel one side of the tape loose, position the wing where you want it, and press the tape back into place.

Illus. 63 gives you a front view of the glider with its wings lifted.

Use this craft indoors or outdoors. Experiment with a paper clip slipped onto the nose to see whether that addition improves the glider's flight.

Now that you've made your first cereal-box glider, why not design one of your own? Experiment with a different type of tail. Make different types of tail sections. Try a new design for the fuselage. Test another type of wing.

Not all your glider designs will fly as well as the one you made here. Some will probably perform better. If one model fails, try to figure out what went wrong and build another, better one.

Indoor Action Flier

To build the *Indoor Action Flier* begin with a sheet of notebook paper, typing paper, or computer paper. Turn the paper into a square, the way you learned back on page 35.

Fold the paper in half so that it looks like Illus. 64.

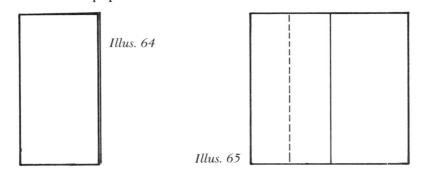

Illus. 64

Illus. 65

Unfold the sheet, and the paper should look like Illus. 65. Fold the paper along the dotted line, so that the edge of the paper comes right to the center fold you just made.

Your *Indoor Action Flier* should look just like Illus. 66, now that you've made this fold.

Illus. 66

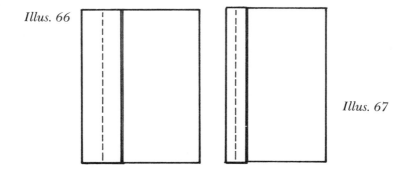

Illus. 67

The dotted line shown in Illus. 66 is your next fold. Once again, fold the paper so that the edge comes right to the center fold.

You've now arrived at Illus. 67. Make one more fold along the dotted line seen in the drawing. Since you're folding several layers of paper at this point take your time and make the fold even. Crease it firmly into place.

You'll get a better crease if you slow down and take your time.

After all these folds your *Flier* should look just like the one in Illus. 68.

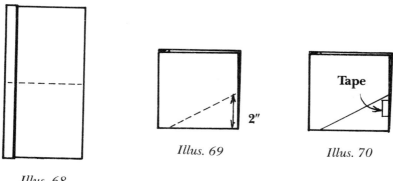

Illus. 69

2″

Tape

Illus. 70

Illus. 68

Fold up the bottom of the paper to the top along the dotted line that appears in Illus. 68. Crease this fold firmly.

Now fold along the dotted line shown in Illus. 69. Before you fold, note that the fold begins on the left at the first center fold you made and have been using as a guideline. This means that you're making the fold in Illus. 69 so that it starts right at the edge of the thick layers of folded paper. The other end of the fold should be exactly 2″ from the bottom of the paper.

After you make this fold, unfold the paper and refold it along the same fold. In other words, fold it towards you first, unfold it, then fold it away from you. This is so the folded triangle will stick straight down in just a second.

Use a short bit of tape to fasten the two sides of the paper together, as shown in Illus. 70.

Now open the wings. They won't open out flat, but they'll stand up a bit because you just taped the rear of the airplane together. Also, the front edge with all those folds will be pulled back at both ends. Illus. 71 shows a top view of the finished *Flier*.

Launch the *Flier* gently. It will probably flutter and crash. If it does, slip a paper clip onto the front of the triangular stabilizer. Illus. 72 shows where the clip should go.

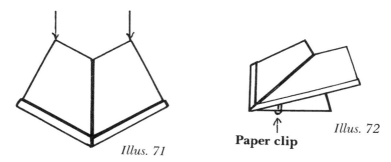

Illus. 71

Paper clip *Illus. 72*

Test it again. This airplane should fly across the room making little "steps" in the air as it goes. If it doesn't perform well, add a second and perhaps even a third paper clip beside the first paper clip.

You may want to bend up the rear wing tips just a bit to see how that changes the way *Flier* performs. The arrows shown in Illus. 71 indicate where to bend the wing tips. Don't fold them, just bend them up a bit.

This airplane reacts strongly to any moving air. It doesn't fly well outside. Even indoors you'll find that it flies differently either facing a draft of air, or flying *with* a little draft.

3
Outdoor Action

The paper action toys in this section all depend upon wind power to make them move and perform. Three of these toys, *Wind Whirler*, *Windwheel* and *Multipart Wind Spinner* can be hung inside near an open window, if you wish. Then, when a breeze comes through the window, they'll perform for you. For the most part, though, the five toys in this chapter are outdoor action toys.

Wind Whirler

Here's another great use for one of those large tubes that come inside big rolls of gift-wrap paper. Begin by cutting off an 8" section of the tube. Take care when you poke the end of your scissors through the tube. Be careful and place a roll of newspapers inside the tube first.

You can see this section of paper tube in Illus. 73. In the drawing are two lines indicating scissor cuts you're going to make.

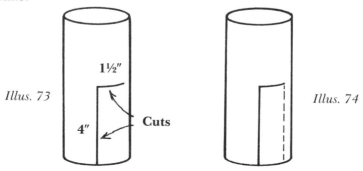

Illus. 73   *Illus. 74*

Make the first cut straight up from the bottom of the tube. This cut should be 4″ long. Then make the second cut at right angles to the first cut. This cut should be anywhere from 1¼″ to 1½″ long.

When this pair of cuts is finished, repeat the process two more times as you work your way around the tube. Try to divide the bottom of the tube into thirds so that your cuts are spaced evenly. If you don't divide the tube exactly into thirds with your cuts, your *Wind Whirler* will still work just fine. Just try to space your three sets of cuts somewhat evenly.

You can measure the outside or circumference of your tube if you wish and divide that number by three. This is obviously the most accurate way to space your cuts.

In Illus. 74 the cuts have been made. The dotted line shows where you're going to fold the cut-out section of material towards you. When the fold is completed, you'll have a curved section of tubing 4″ by 1½″, standing out at right angles from the rest of the tube. Fold very carefully and don't hurry. It takes just a bit of care to make a nice straight fold when you're folding cardboard tubing.

Once the fold is in place, repeat the folding process with the other two sets of cuts.

To make your *Wind Whirler* interesting and attractive, give it some color. Felt-tip markers work well on tubing, as do paints and crayons. With crayons it helps if you fill the inside of the tube with a roll of newspapers, so you won't smash in one side of the tube if you happen to press down too hard.

Make the main part of the *Wind Whirler* one color, and then paint the flaps a contrasting color. Or, paint the right side of the flaps one color and the opposite side another color.

If you have some glitter around, spread a light coat of glue on one or both sides of the flaps and sprinkle glitter on it.

When the wind turns your *Wind Whirler*, the toy will flash and sparkle as it spins.

To hang your finished *Whirler* you'll need two pieces of string. Cut the first piece about 8″ or 9″ long. You're going to fasten both ends of this string to the top edge of the *Whirler*. Carefully poke holes on opposite sides of the *Whirler* and down about ½″ from the top. Tie the ends of the string into these holes and the hard part is done.

You can use either masking tape or mailing tape to hold the string. If you do, place the ends of the string inside the tube and slap on a 2″ piece of tape and press it firmly into place over about 1″ or so of the string's end.

Once you've secured the string in place, cut off another piece of string long enough to hang the finished whirler from a hook on the porch, from a tree branch, or wherever you've decided to place the toy. Illus. 75 shows the finished *Whirler* with its hanging strings in place.

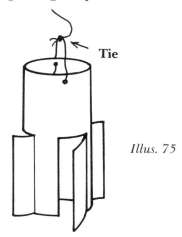

Tie

Illus. 75

This is an outdoor action toy because that's where the wind is. If you wish, however, hang it in an open window, where it can catch the breeze.

Wind Sock

While you're dealing with large cardboard tubing, cut off a chunk of gift-wrap tubing about 4″ long. This is going to be the main part of the body of a *Wind Sock*.

You'll want to paint or color your *Wind Sock* to make it more interesting. You can simply use felt-tip marker, paint, or crayon and color it one solid color. You might want to add a second coat of large dots or stripes over the solid color.

If you want to be a little fancier, think of your wind sock as some sort of creature. Give it large eyes, and perhaps a mouth full of sharp teeth. Just use your imagination and come up with an exciting design for the body of your *Wind Sock*. Illus. 76 shows several possibilities.

 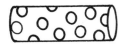 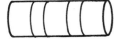

Illus. 76

If you're making your *Wind Sock* before Halloween, paint it white. Then, by using white plastic for its tail (in just a minute), you'll have created a ghostly figure that will flutter nicely in the evening breeze.

To make a tail for your *Wind Sock*, the best possible material is lightweight plastic cut from a grocery bag. The colored plastic wrapper the morning newspaper comes in on rainy days is absolutely perfect. The plastic grocery bag from the supermarket is great, especially if you need a white tail for a ghostly figure.

Cut eight or ten strips of plastic about 1¼″ or 1½″ wide. Make the strips about 2′ or so in length (this is about the length of a newspaper wrapper). If you're using a bag from the supermarket, cut the bag along both sides and flatten it out. This gives you strips of plastic *Wind Sock* tail that are twice as long as the bag was originally.

If your scissors are really sharp, all you need to do to cut these strips is to make a little cut and then just pull the plastic towards you. The sharp scissors blade will cut the thin plastic without your having to cut your way along the length of the container.

Use plastic tail strips of different colors, and then alternate the colors when you attach them to the *Wind Sock*'s body. Alternate red, white, and blue tail strips if you want to make a *Wind Sock* reminding people of the United States flag. In this case, paint the body with the same colors.

To attach the tail strips to the body of the *Wind Sock* use strips of masking tape or mailing tape. Narrow cellophane tape will work, if you don't have the other types of tape, but the *Wind Sock* will hang out in the wind, and it needs really strong, sticky tape for best results.

Don't be tempted to rip off a long strip of tape. It's easier to cut off a short chunk of tape and attach one tail strip, and then move on to the next strip of plastic. Illus. 77 shows two tail strips already in place.

Illus. 77

Tape

Space the plastic tail strips evenly and work your way around the base of the body. Then, if you wish, you can use one or two long strips of tape to go all the way around the body on top of the short pieces of tape you've already used.

If you don't have plastic material available, you can use strips of paper or cloth. If you use notebook paper or typing paper, you'll need to glue or tape two shorter strips together to make a longer tail strip. Both paper and cloth work well, but they're heavier than plastic, which means that the wind has to blow harder in order to make the strips stand out and flutter properly.

To hang the *Wind Sock*, you need to carefully poke a hole at the top of the body about ½" or even 1" from the end of the tube. Cut off enough strong string so that you can hang the *Wind Sock* from a tree branch, from the top of the porch, or anywhere the wind can get to it.

Check Illus. 78 to see how the hanging string looks once it's tied firmly onto the finished *Wind Sock*.

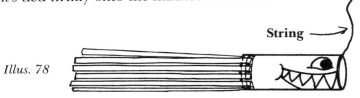

String

Illus. 78

When the wind blows, your *Wind Sock* will turn so that the body faces the wind. The tail strips will flutter out from behind the *Sock*. The stronger the wind blows, the more the tail strips will flutter and flop. You'll also find that as the wind blows stronger, the body of your *Wind Sock* will tip, so that the rear of the body rises. In a really strong wind, this action toy will stand almost horizontally as the air passes through the hollow body and keeps the tail standing straight out behind it.

Make several of these interesting outdoor toys with different designs. They're fun to watch and they're bound to attract attention.

Growler

You'll see how the *Growler* got its name after you make it and play with it for the first time.

This outside toy was a popular toy that your great-grandparents might have played with, especially if they lived in rural areas.

Begin by cutting three strips of cereal-box material about 12″ long and 1½″ wide. Make sure all three strips are exactly the same size.

Make a scissor cut about 2″ long in one end of a strip of material. This cut is shown in Illus. 79.

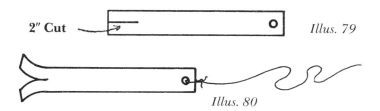

2″ Cut

Illus. 79

Illus. 80

Now carefully poke a hole in the other end of the cardboard strip about 1″ from the end. This hole is also shown in Illus. 79.

Use this piece of material as a pattern so you can make similar cuts and holes in the other two strips. Make certain the cuts and holes in all three strips line up exactly.

You can either glue or tape the three strips together to form one thick strip of cereal-box material, with a cut in one end and a hole in the other. If you use tape instead of glue, don't use narrow cellophane tape. Masking tape is great, and so is mailing tape. If you glue the three strips together, place them under a book or something fairly heavy until the glue is completely dry.

When the glue is dry, bend up one side next to the cut so it sticks up about ½″. Bend the opposite side down the same distance. Illus. 80 shows how the two narrow ends of material should look.

Nice hole poking! Did you remember to line them up?

Cut off a piece of strong string or cord about 4' long. Tie a loop in one end. This loop will fit over your thumb when you play with *Growler*. Push the other end of the string through the hole and tie it with a firm knot. The string with its end loop is also shown in Illus. 80.

Take *Growler* outside. Slip the looped end of the string over your thumb. Get a firm grip on the string next to the loop with the rest of your hand. The loop over your thumb is just a safety measure to make certain you don't let the *Growler* slip away and fly free.

Make sure you're standing at least 10' from any person or any object. Raise your hand above your head and begin to swing *Growler* in a circle over your head. Spin it faster and faster and listen to the sound it makes. Now you know how *Growler* got its name. It sounds a lot like a helicopter trying to take off.

Growler is strictly an outdoor toy. Don't ever spin it close to other people.

Windwheel

The *Windwheel* you're about to make is formed from two pieces. It's basically an outdoor hanging toy, but it can be hung in an open window.

An outdoor *Windwheel* should be constructed from file-folder material, or perhaps the stiff cover of the special advertising section of a magazine. An indoor *Windwheel* can be made from notebook paper or computer paper.

For your first *Windwheel*, use notebook paper, because it's easy to work with and it will let you see how the finished product looks. Then you can decide if you wish to enlarge your next *Windwheel* to take outside.

Begin with a piece of material at least 8″ by 5″. Place the sheet of material as shown in Illus. 81. Draw the three lines seen in the upper left-hand corner of the material.

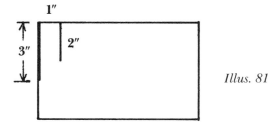

Illus. 81

Start by drawing the 3″ vertical line at the left side of the material. Then draw the 1″ line, which extends from the top

of the line you first drew. Finally, draw a 2″ line vertically, down from the end of the 1″ line.

Now draw the two 7″ horizontal lines, shown in Illus. 82. Make certain these lines are at right angles to the vertical lines you drew a few seconds ago.

Finish the drawing by adding the 2″ and 3″ vertical lines seen in the lower right-hand part of the drawing in Illus. 83.

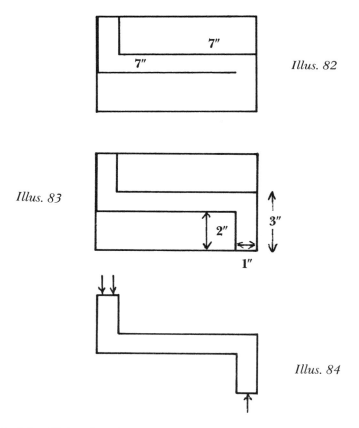

Illus. 82

Illus. 83

Illus. 84

Finish off the drawing by connecting these last two vertical lines with a 1″ horizontal line.

Cut out the *Windwheel* piece you've just drawn. Use it as a pattern and draw another one exactly like it.

Place one piece in front of you, so that it looks just like the one shown in Illus. 84.

Pull up the lower right-hand end (indicated by one arrow) so that it overlaps the upper left-hand end (shown with two arrows) about ½″. Fasten these two ends together with tape. The *Windwheel* piece should look like the one shown in Illus. 85.

Set this piece aside and do exactly the same thing with the other piece of material. When you've done this, you'll have two pieces that look just like the one shown in Illus. 85.

Slip one piece inside the other so you have a four-pointed *Windwheel*. Illus. 86 gives you a top view of your project.

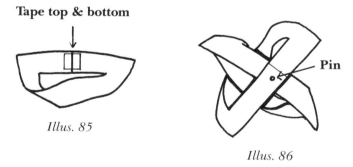

Tape top & bottom

Illus. 85

Pin

Illus. 86

Tape the two sections together, making sure the two *Windwheel* pieces are at right angles to one another.

To test your *Windwheel*, push a straight pin through the middle of the point at which the two pieces overlap. Push the pin point into the eraser end of a pencil, as shown in Illus. 87. Now, either walk rapidly, or take your *Windwheel* out into the breeze. It should spin nicely for you.

Just for fun, take your *Windwheel* off its pencil mounting and remove the pin. Turn the *Windwheel* over and push the pin through the exact middle of the opposite side where the two pieces cross one another. Push the pin again into the eraser end of your pencil.

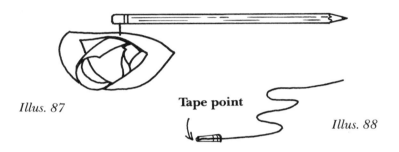

Illus. 87   **Tape point**   *Illus. 88*

Now when you walk rapidly or the wind blows, you'll see that your *Windwheel* turns in the opposite direction. Keep this thought in mind. You may want to use it a few minutes from now.

To make your *Windwheel* a permanent outdoor toy, mount it on a string. Cut off enough string so you can hang the *Windwheel* and still have enough string to anchor it at the bottom. One way to anchor the string is to tie a fairly heavy weight onto the bottom end of the string. Another is to tie the bottom end of the string to a porch rail, or something like that.

Use a pin or an awl (if you have one) to enlarge the holes you already made in the middle of the *Windwheel*. These holes need to be big enough for the string to go through.

Before you try to thread the string through the *Windwheel*, make a little tape point on the string. Cut off ½" or a bit more of tape. Wrap it around one end of the string, as shown in Illus. 88.

Make sure the tape comes to a point. Use this point of tape to push through the holes so you can hang your *Windwheel* on the piece of string.

Once you've threaded the *Windwheel* onto the string, decide exactly how far down the string you want the wheel to hang. Tie a big knot in the string at this point, and then slide the *Windwheel* down the string, until it rests on the knot, as shown in Illus. 89.

Illus. 89

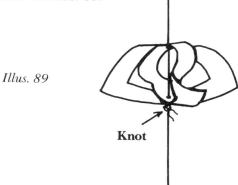

Knot

You can hang your *Windwheel* either outside, or in an open window, and it will become a longtime spinning toy.

Now that you see how the two-piece *Windwheel* is made and how it works, it's time to get serious about this toy.

To make this toy more interesting, paint or color the two arms; do this before you begin bending and taping. Think about making the opposite sides of each arm different colors. You can color or paint both pieces the same or differently; that's up to you.

How about placing two or three *Windwheels* on the same string? Just remember to tie a big knot in the string before you thread on another *Windwheel*.

For a special effect, turn over one of the *Windwheels* so it will blow in a reverse direction. Depending upon the force of the breeze or wind, you'll end up with wheels blowing in different directions at the same time, or one wheel barely moving while the one above or below it spins nicely. This makes a really interesting wind toy.

Illus. 90 shows two wheels on the same string with one wheel reversed.

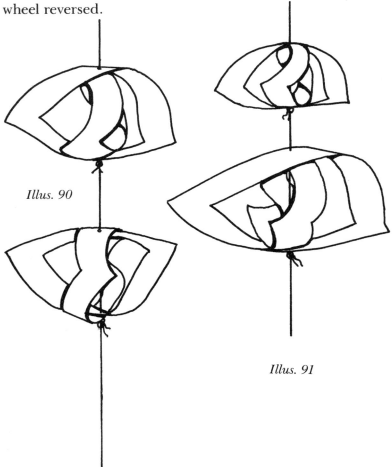

Illus. 90

Illus. 91

For variety, make one wheel larger than the other, as shown in Illus. 91. Of course, you can still reverse one of the wheels as well.

Illus. 92 shows the measurements for a larger *Windwheel*. When making a wheel this large, you'll need stiff material, such as a file-folder; otherwise the arms are likely to flop around and do a poor job.

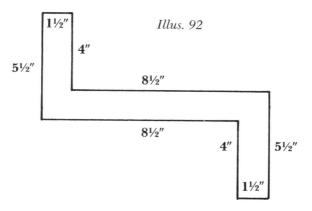

Illus. 92

Note that this wheel's arms are 1½″ wide, instead of 1″ for the smaller wheel you made first. Draw the lines in the same order as you did before, and assemble the larger wheel just as you did the first smaller one.

If you wish, you can make a *Windwheel* that is in between the sizes of the two you've just made; merely adjust the measurements a bit. You can construct an even larger one, as well, if you have material of the right size.

Remember to always make the mounting holes exactly in the middle, where the arms cross. Don't forget to tie that big knot in the string to keep the wheels from slipping down to the bottom.

Multipart Wind Spinner

This wind toy is basically an outdoor toy. However, if you make it with lightweight material and hang it in a breezy place, it, too, will work inside.

Let's make your first *Multipart Wind Spinner* out of fairly stiff material, so that it's suitable for an outdoor action toy. Begin by cutting nine or ten strips of file-folder material, or perhaps the stiff advertising pages from a magazine. These strips should be 1½" wide, and as long as the material.

If you use stiff advertising pages, or cover pages from magazines, they'll provide their own color. When you use an old file-folder for your strips of material, color or paint them before making the *Wind Spinner*. Look ahead at the illustrations before coloring the strips. Decide if you want each part of the *Wind Spinner* a different color, or the outsides of each strip one color and the inside parts another color. Don't begin painting or coloring until you read the next paragraph.

You're going to join strips together to make the four parts of the *Wind Spinner*. Glue or masking tape will work just fine. However, don't color or paint the strips until you've glued or taped them to the proper length. Glue and even tape won't always hold on a waxy surface after you've colored it. Some paints tend to peel off when tape is applied over them.

There are four sections in this *Wind Spinner*. One is 15" long. The second is 22" long. The third strip needs to be 27" long and the final strip should be 30" long. If you make other *Wind Spinners*, you may adjust the lengths of the strips by making them shorter or longer to suit your taste.

When you glue or tape two strips together to form a longer strip, it's best to overlap the two strips at least ½". If you use tape rather than glue, tape both sides of the overlap so that you don't have a loose end that can get bent or flop around.

If you end up with a strip a bit shorter or longer than the length suggested above, don't worry about it. Your *Wind Spinner* will still work just fine.

Once you've spliced and cut the strips to the proper

Wrap the tape around the two strips
of paper—not me!

length, assemble your *Wind Spinner*. Your first step is to form
each strip of material into a ring. Glue or tape the ends
together firmly so that each ring looks like the one shown in
Illus. 93.

Cut a piece of string long enough to hang the finished *Wind Spinner*. Tie a large knot in the string at the point you want the top of the *Wind Spinner* to be located.

Now take a short piece of tape and wrap it tightly around one end of the string to form a little point to make it easier to thread the string through the strips of material. Do the same with the other end of the string. Illus. 94 shows the knotted string and the taped points.

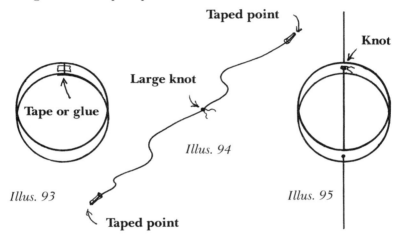

Taped point

Knot

Large knot

Tape or glue

Illus. 94

Illus. 93

Illus. 95

Taped point

Use an awl (if you have one) to make a hole right in the middle of one side of the small circle. If you don't have an awl, use a straight pin and rotate the pin round and round to enlarge the hole, so that the string can go through it. Now thread the top end of string through the hole you just made. Slip the circle down on the string until it rests against the big knot you made earlier.

Illus. 95 shows the smallest circle already in place on the string.

Do the same with the other three circles, threading them onto the string in size order. Once all four circles are on the string, tie another large knot just above the circles, as shown in Illus. 96. This will prevent the circles from slipping up the string. Leave just a bit of space between the top of the largest circle and this knot, so that the loops have room to turn on the string.

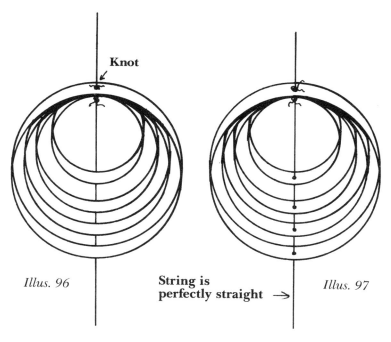

Knot

Illus. 96

String is perfectly straight →

Illus. 97

Your next step is to make holes for the string in the bottoms of each of the four circles. These holes must be in an absolutely straight line with one another. If even one hole is out of line, it will cause the string to bind that circle, as well as the ones above and below it, and it will act as a brake.

Illus. 97 shows how the string has already been threaded through the four circles.

Take the finished *Wind Spinner* outside and let it catch a breeze. You can mount it from a tree branch or from a porch, or from any other suitable place. To keep the *Spinner* from flying off to one side, anchor it at the bottom as well as at the top. You can either tie the bottom down or hang a weight from it.

If you want to make a *Wind Spinner* for your room, use notebook paper or typing paper, because it takes less breeze to spin the lighter-weight spinner.

4
Indoor Action Toys

The toys in this section can be used outdoors as well as indoors, but you'll probably end up playing with them inside more often. *Jaws* and *Funny Face* are fantastic toys to make and use to entertain small children. They're just as much fun to make and use as puppet faces whose mouths open and whose faces move as you speak for them.

The final toy in the group is actually a construction set to which you can add piece after piece at any time. It's a great toy to return to time after time whenever you get the urge to build and create.

Jaws

Jaws is a quickly made little critter that you hold in one hand. It's fun to play with, and it takes about a minute to make. You can use it just as a novelty action toy, or you could put words into its mouth and have *Jaws* become a little hand puppet.

Begin with a piece of file-card or folder material about 2½″ by 4″. Extremely stiff paper will work, but regular notebook paper or typing paper isn't stiff enough to make *Jaws*.

Place the material on top of a pad of newspaper on your desk or table. Now use your ruler and a ballpoint pen to make the line shown in Illus. 98. This line should be about 2″ long. This leaves one inch at both the top and bottom of the line, between it and the end of the card.

Push down good and hard on the ballpoint pen, because you want this line to be a deep crease or groove in the material. Instead of using a ballpoint pen, you could use a dull table knife to make this crease. Just hold the knife right near the tip and draw the line with the knife's tip.

Be sure you have a pad of newspaper under the material while doing this. If you score a groove in the table, you'll be in trouble!

Here comes the tricky part. Hold the card as shown in Illus. 99.

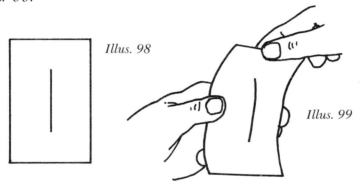

Illus. 98

Illus. 99

Press your thumb and fingers towards each other slightly but firmly. At the same time, use your other hand to bend the top of the card forward. Don't fold it! Just bend it forward while pushing together with your other thumb and fingers.

What you want to have happen is for the top of the card to bend down, so when you squeeze the sides of the card together and then release them, the top of the card will move up and down.

Illus. 100 shows how the top of the card bends forward as the sides are squeezed together.

As soon as the top of the card is performing properly, deal with the bottom. Do it just the way you did the top. Maintain pressure on the sides of the card and use your other hand to bend the bottom of the card upwards.

When both the bottom and the top of the card are working correctly, *Jaws* should look like Illus. 101.

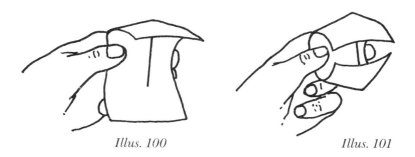

Illus. 100   *Illus. 101*

By squeezing the sides of the card together, both jaws close. You can pick up small items with *Jaws*, or just use *Jaws* as a talking hand puppet.

You can color the inside of *Jaws'* mouth red or pink. Add a bit of color on both the top and bottom edge, and *Jaws* has lipstick.

You can add eyes to *Jaws* by making the two U-shaped cuts shown in Illus. 102.

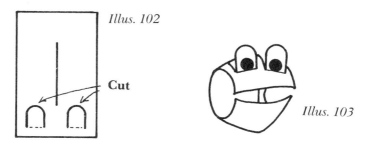

Illus. 102

Cut

Illus. 103

If you do this, place the card on the newspaper pad when you poke the end of your scissors through the material. Don't poke your finger! Once you have a small hole in the card, use just the tips of the scissors in tiny snips to cut out the "U" shapes.

When the cuts are made, color in pupils for *Jaws'* eyes. Then fold up the two little U-shaped sections. Illus. 103 gives a front view of *Jaws* with its eyes colored and folded into place.

You can make *Jaws* with a pointed or curved mouth. Illus. 104 shows two ways you can cut the file card or other stiff material to give this little action toy a different look. When you do this, keep the main part of *Jaws* 4″ long and add length for the curved or pointed part of its mouth or beak.

Illus. 104

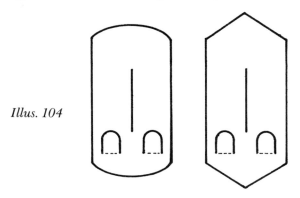

Since *Jaws'* bulging eyes remind most people of a frog or a toad, you might want to use some green color to make *Jaws* look more like these animals.

Funny Face

This paper action toy gives you a great little hand puppet with a flapping jaw, which you can control as you speak for it. It's also a great toy to use when entertaining young children.

Begin with a square sheet of notebook or typing paper. If necessary, glance back at page 35 to see how to change a rectangular piece of paper into a square.

Fold the paper in half and then unfold it. This gives you the center fold that is already in place in Illus. 105.

In Illus. 105 there are two dotted lines. Fold down both corners along these dotted lines so that the edges of the folded corners come right to the center fold.

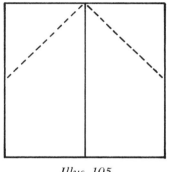
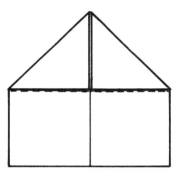

Illus. 105　　　　　*Illus. 106*

Once these folds are in place, *Funny Face* looks like the drawing in Illus. 106.

Your next step is to fold down the pointed end of the paper along the dotted line shown in Illus. 106. This fold will end up with the point just touching the bottom edge of the paper. You can see the results in Illus. 107.

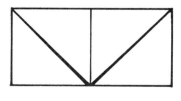
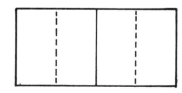

Illus. 107　　　　　*Illus. 108*

Once your project looks like Illus. 107, turn it over. Now it looks like Illus. 108.

The dotted lines in Illus. 108 tell you that you're going to fold both sides in until they touch the center fold. Do that now.

Once these two folds are finished, *Funny Face* appears as shown in Illus. 109. The dotted lines in the drawing indicate two more folds you're going to make.

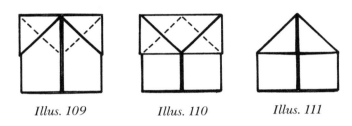

Illus. 109   *Illus. 110*   *Illus. 111*

Fold down each corner along the dotted line in Illus. 109. When you finish the two folds, *Funny Face* looks like the drawing in Illus. 110.

Make the two folds along the dotted lines in Illus. 110. Crease these folds well. Once this is done, your project should look like Illus. 111.

Now that you've done a fine job of folding and creasing, unfold the two folds you just made, so that you're back to Illus. 110, except that instead of dotted lines, you have folds in place. Illus. 112 shows this step.

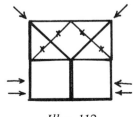

Illus. 112

There are two arrows shown at the top of Illus. 112. These arrows indicate the corners you're going to turn inside out with your next fold.

To make it easier to turn these corners inside out, locate the folds marked with "X"s in Illus. 112. Fold these folds backwards and crease them. Then fold them forward again so that they look just like Illus. 112. This backward folding is just to make the paper limber and easier to deal with.

Begin with the right-hand side. Hold the project with one hand as shown by the double arrows at the right of the drawing. Then push in with the other hand on the single arrow so that the corner reverses itself, or turns inside out. The upper right-hand corner indicated by the single arrow is now hidden between the front and the back of the paper.

Look ahead to Illus. 113. Once you've turned the upper right-hand corner inside out, as described above, your *Funny Face* will look like the right-hand half of Illus. 113.

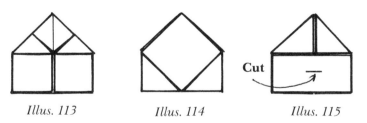

Illus. 113   *Illus. 114*   *Illus. 115*

Now do the same with the left-hand side of the project, and it will look exactly like the drawing in Illus. 113.

Turn over *Funny Face* and it looks like Illus. 114.

Set this paper aside for just a minute and grab your scissors and a piece of cereal-box cardboard. Cut a strip about ⅝″ wide and 8″ long. Once this is done, go back to the folded paper.

Lift up *Funny Face*'s lower jaw so that things look like Illus. 115. The lower jaw is the pointed part of the paper shown by the arrow in Illus. 114. Fold the lower jaw so it will stay up, as shown in Illus. 115.

With the jaw folded up and out of the way, make a cut ⅝″ wide, as shown in the illustration. Make the cut about 1″ up from the bottom of the paper. This cut is made *only* in the top layer of paper; don't cut the bottom layers of paper.

Now push the strip of cardboard up through the cut you just made, so it looks like Illus. 116. Keep pushing the cardboard strip upwards until it's all the way into the triangle of folded paper. You'll see you're pushing the cardboard strip into the triangle of folded paper that is under the lower jaw you folded up out of the way just a minute ago.

Once the cardboard strip is in place, fold down the bottom corners of *Funny Face* along the dotted lines seen in Illus. 117. Be sure to crease these folds well so they stay in place.

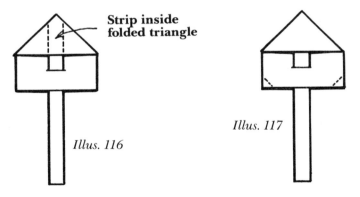

Strip inside folded triangle

Illus. 116

Illus. 117

Now fold both triangles forward so they stick out like jaws or a beak. Draw or paint a pair of big eyes on the two little triangles which stick up, as seen in Illus. 118.

Hold *Funny Face* at the lower corner, as shown in Illus. 118. To make the lower jaw move, just move the strip of cardboard up and down. As you do this, the lower jaw will open and close.

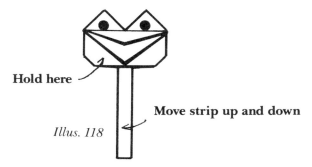

Hold here

Move strip up and down

Illus. 118

If you wish, paint the inside of the mouth pink or red. This makes the moving lower jaw more interesting.

Now that you've got *Funny Face*'s lower jaw moving, it's up to you what words you put into its mouth. Just don't let *Funny Face* say anything to get you into trouble!

Magic Wand

A carefully constructed *Magic Wand* will give you loads of fun. You'll want to play with this paper action toy again and again.

Begin by rolling a sheet of notebook paper or computer paper into a tight roll, so that you end up with a paper tube as long as the sheet of paper was wide. In other words, roll the sheet of paper so that your tube is as long as the short side of the paper.

Use several strips of tape to hold the roll together, as shown in Illus. 119. This is the handle for your *Magic Wand*. Once it's taped firmly together, set it aside for a few minutes.

Tape

Illus. 119

Now cut some strips of fairly stiff paper. A good grade of computer paper will work just fine, as will stiff typing paper or heavy notebook paper. Really thin paper just won't do the job.

Cut three sheets of paper the long way, so you have a total of nine strips of paper about 3″ wide and nearly a foot long. If you cut them just a bit less than 3″ wide, you can get three strips from each sheet of paper.

Now comes the step in which you need to be firm but careful. Grasp one strip of paper, so you're holding one end in each hand; Illus. 120 shows how.

Place one end of the paper against the square edge of a kitchen counter, or a table. Now, holding the paper firmly in both hands, pull the paper down firmly over the edge of the counter or table. Illus. 121 shows how this is done.

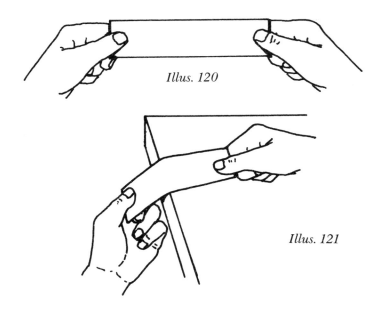

Illus. 120

Illus. 121

Don't pull so hard so you rip the paper. If you do, just discard that strip and cut another. After pulling the paper

Some people just don't know their own strength!

across the edge of the counter, let go of it. It should curl around in a circle. This is exactly what you want to happen.

Now do the same with the two other strips of paper. All this pulling and curling will make the paper strips curl up instead of lying flat.

Tape

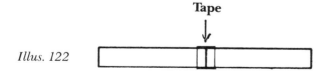

Illus. 122

You'll need some cellophane tape or masking tape now.

Place two strips end-to-end and tape them together, as shown in Illus. 122. You'll have to flatten out the curl as you do this. The best way to do this is to put the strip down on the table so it wants to curl into the table instead of up into the air; this will make taping easier.

Make sure you tape the strips of paper so the curls are all going in the same direction. If you press each strip down so it tries to curl into the table, everything should work perfectly.

Tape both sides of the joint where the two strips meet. If you can handle the tape without having it stick to itself, tear off a strip of tape long enough to do one side and then fold around and do the second side as well. If the long tape is a problem, just use two shorter strips of tape.

Now add another strip of paper to one end of the pair you just taped together. Tape it on just as you did before.

Keep adding the rest of the strips until you have a long strip of paper about 3″ wide and nearly 6′ long. It looks like Illus. 123.

Illus. 123

Now it's time to tape this long, narrow strip of paper onto the handle you made earlier. Use a strip of tape as shown in Illus. 124. Just make sure the long strip of paper wants to curl around the handle. That's the whole point in doing all that paper pulling before.

Begin turning the handle until the entire strip of paper is wound around it, like the drawing shown in Illus. 125. Hold onto the loose end and keep turning the handle until the strip is tightly wound around the handle.

Now wrap a rubber band around the strip so that it looks like Illus. 126.

Leave the *Magic Wand* with the rubber band around it overnight, to make sure the paper will hold its curl.

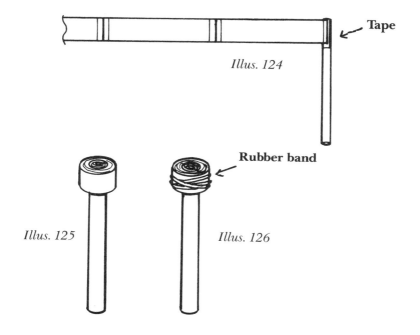

Illus. 124

Rubber band

Illus. 125　　　　*Illus. 126*

Tape

Illus. 127

To use the *Magic Wand*, remove the rubber band. The tightly wound paper strip will loosen a bit when you do this. That's fine, it's supposed to.

Grasp the end of the wand firmly in your hand, with the wand pointing towards the ceiling. Give your wrist a sharp snap so the wand points away from you.

The *Magic Wand* will stretch out so it looks like Illus. 127.

After the wand has stretched out, lift your wrist so that the wand points upwards. The paper strip will rewind itself and it'll be ready for another snap. Practise a bit, and you'll see how this works. The trick is to give a sharp snap of the wrist but not to snap it hard enough so the end of the paper strip comes unrolled. By the time you've practised a few snaps, you'll have no problems.

The wand is a great paper action toy because you can snap it out and have it come back time after time. If the end happens to slip so it's hanging out, just wrap it back into place.

When you're through playing with your *Magic Wand*, wrap the paper tightly and slip the rubber band around it. This helps preserve its ability to curl and return.

Do not point the wand towards anyone's face when you're playing with it.

If you wish, add another three or even six strips of paper to your *Magic Wand*. This will give you a lot more distance when you snap your wrist.

You can use crayons or felt-tip markers to brighten up your *Magic Wand* and make it a real eye-catcher.

After you've played with your wand you'll see why it's popular with English children, who buy such wands ready-made in street markets.

Action Construction

Here's a perfect use for all those cardboard tubes, such as those found in the center of toilet-tissue rolls and inside gift-wrap paper. This *Action Construction* set is one you can play with time and time again and add to as you have more tubes available to turn into building cylinders.

A cylinder is just a round, hollow form. It can be a tube from the inside of a roll of paper towels, or even a rolled-up piece of paper.

Let's begin by making a pattern or template for the square, which is an important part of this set of construction materials. Illus. 128 shows the plan for this square.

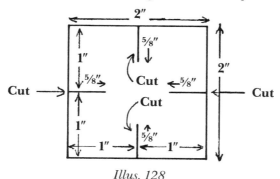

Illus. 128

Begin with a piece of cereal-box material 2″ on all sides. Halfway between each pair of corners draw a line ⅝″ long. Since this line is halfway between the corners, it's exactly 1″ from each corner. Be absolutely certain this ⅝″ line is at right angles to the side of the material. Carefully cut each ⅝″ line with your scissors.

Now cut ten or so 2″ squares from cereal-box material. Use the pattern (which is called a *template*) you just cut and measured to locate the cuts in each of the new squares. Just place your template on top of a 2″ by 2″ square and use a pencil to draw the four cut lines on the new square. This way you only have to do all that measuring once. After you've drawn the four cut lines, cut them with your scissors.

Let's make the cylinders that will interlock with the squares to form your *Action Construction* pieces. Cut a cylinder 2″ high from the end of a paper tube. You can see such a cylinder in Illus. 129.

The cylinder in the illustration is 2″ in diameter; that's 2″ across. This is a perfect size for building cylinders. However, you'll probably have paper tubes that are larger and smaller than two inches across. They'll do just fine. Just follow along and learn how to locate the cuts that turn the piece of tubing into an action building block. You'll learn how to make adjustments for tubes larger or smaller than the one shown in the drawing.

Notice in Illus. 129 that there are eight slots cut in the top of the cylinder and eight more in the bottom. If your tube is smaller than this, you'll end up with fewer slots. Also notice the slots in the top are in a direct line with those cut in the bottom. This is very important!

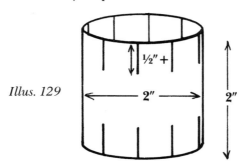

Illus. 129

The slots need to be spaced evenly in order for your cylinder to become a good building block. Here's how to do it. Begin by cutting one slot along the top of the cylinder. It should be just a fraction more than ½″ deep.

Cut the second slot on the opposite side of the cylinder so it's exactly straight across from the first slot. Illus. 130 shows how things look at this point.

Cut the next slot exactly midway between the two you already cut. Position the fourth slot directly across from the third. This will locate it halfway between the first pair of slots. Illus. 131 shows things at this point.

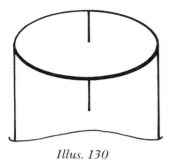

Illus. 130

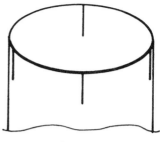

Illus. 131

If your cylinder is 2″ in diameter or larger, you have room for four more slots along the top. If it's smaller, like a tube from inside a roll of paper towels or toilet tissue, stop cutting slots along the top of the cylinder, and move on to the bottom.

For cylinders 2″ in diameter or larger, locate one slot halfway between each pair of slots you've already cut. This means you'll cut four more slots, and end up with the top of your cylinder looking like the one shown in Illus. 129.

Finish the cylinder by turning it over and cutting the bottom slots so each slot is directly below a slot in the top.

What happens if you don't have cardboard tubes exactly two inches across, or you have tubes of all sizes? The answer is simple; we'll work with what's available.

For tubes larger than 2″, you can cut more than eight slots around the edge. Say your tube is 3″ in diameter. Locate the

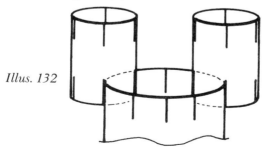

Illus. 132

first four slots just as you did in Illus. 131. In this case, cut *two* slots between each pair of slots, instead of cutting just one slot per pair.

As soon as you have a dozen cylinders to go with your square pieces, it's time to experiment. Illus. 132 shows how these pieces interlock.

Slip the slot in the bottom of a cylinder into a slot in the top of another cylinder. If you find the slots fit too snugly, you can trim them just a fraction larger with your scissors.

Now try using the squares to connect the cylinders. Just interlock a top slot in a square with the slot in a ring. Now interlock a bottom slot in the square with another ring. Work with these action building blocks for just a minute and you'll quickly find out how they work. You can even crisscross the squares, if you wish.

You'll need more than a dozen cylinders. The batch you just made will let you see how to build, but they won't go very far. The thing to do is to make a few more pieces each time you build with this set. That way you won't spend all your time making pieces and no time playing with them.

You may wonder why you didn't make a pattern or template for the cylinders as you did for the squares, since the

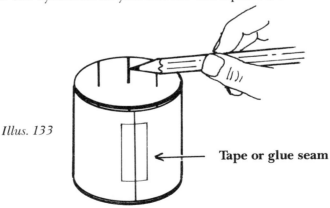

Illus. 133

Tape or glue seam

template saves so much time. If you're using lots of tubes the same size a template will work. If your tubes are all different sizes, it's just about as quick to cut each cylinder separately.

In case you have many cylinders the same size, here's how to use a sheet of paper to make a template. Wrap a piece of paper around a finished cylinder, as shown in Illus. 133.

Glue or tape the loose end so it won't unroll when it is removed from the cylinder. Make certain the paper for the template is loose enough so that you can slip it off the cylinder.

Mark each slot from the inside of the cylinder. See how the pencil is positioned in Illus. 133.

Remove the template and cut out the slots for both the top and the bottom. To use the template, just slip it over a fresh cylinder, mark the slots with a pencil or a ballpoint pen, then remove the template. Carefully cut the slots, and your cylinder is finished.

If you want to put some variety into this set of construction pieces, make a few squares like the one shown in Illus. 134.

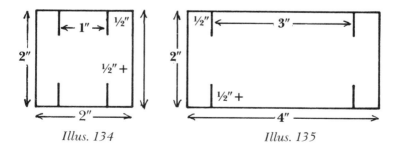

Illus. 134   *Illus. 135*

Note that the slots are cut ½″ from each side, and there are two slots at the top and bottom, but no slots on the sides.

For a still different building piece, add a few rectangles, such as the one shown in Illus. 135.

Check the measurements carefully. If either the new square or the rectangle appeal to you, measure and cut one of each for a template. Then make a few of these variety building pieces and see how you like them.

You can also make half-cylinders if you wish; they look like the one shown in Illus. 136.

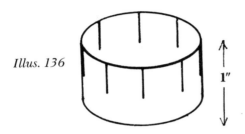

Illus. 136

1"

Since this cylinder is only 1" high, you'll make slots only along the top.

You probably have wondered about the possibility of making cylinders from flat material. It can be done, but it's a little tricky.

If you want to try turning a piece of cereal-box material into a cylinder, here's how. Cut a strip 2" wide and 7" long. This will make a cylinder 2" in diameter while leaving a little over ½" as a flap to glue or tape into place.

Be careful not to fold or crease the cardboard when you form it into a cylinder. If you have a strong cylinder, such as a food can, to wrap the cardboard strip around that's great. If not, use your thumbs and forefingers to form the cardboard into a curved strip. What you're doing at this point is making many, many tiny creases or bends in the material.

File-folder material is easier to make into cylinders than is the heavier cereal-box material. You can help turn a strip of such material into a cylinder by pulling it over the edge of a kitchen counter, just as you did with the strips for the *Magic Wand* back on page 87.

Avoid getting a large crease or fold in the strip. If that happens, straighten the fold and keep on making the little bends with your hands.

When it comes to taping or gluing, tape is easier to handle. If you use glue, here's a hint. Once the glue is applied, place a pair of paper clips along the seam to hold things together until the glue dries. Illus. 137 shows how this is done.

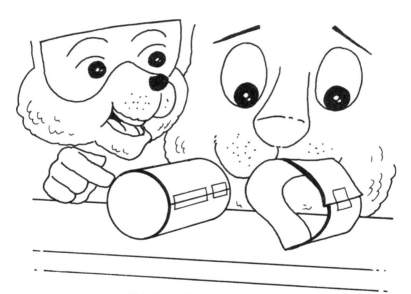

This is a cylinder! Yours looks more like a sculpture!

If tubes are available, use them. Making cylinders from flat material is a slow job.

If you want to put a bit of variety into your building blocks, take a look at Illus. 138.

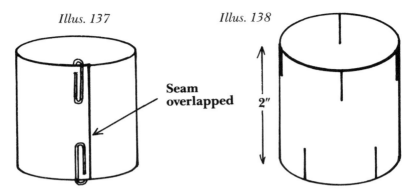

Illus. 137   *Illus. 138*

Seam overlapped   2″

The cylinder in Illus. 138 has been cut from the core of a roll of paper towels. Therefore, it has only four slots each at the top and at the bottom. However, as you can see, the slots in the bottom don't come directly under those at the top. They're spaced so that the bottom slots are halfway between each pair of top slots.

This different approach to locating the bottom slots in a cylinder gives your construction a different look. Each time you add a new layer of cylinders, they will be offset a bit.

You can go for larger cylinders by using the cardboard from round containers for food products such as salt and breakfast cereals. Use the distance between the four slots in a paper-towel or toilet-tissue roll as a guide, and try to cut the slots in the larger material about the same distance apart.

If you happen to end up with some slots in any cylinders closer or farther apart than in other cylinders, don't worry. The small difference won't hurt your construction at all.

Illus. 139 shows how you can begin interlocking cylinders with other cylinders to begin construction using cylinders only.

For more variety, make a few cylinders 1½″ high and others 3″ high. Illus. 140 shows cylinders 1″ in height, 1½″ high, and 3″ tall.

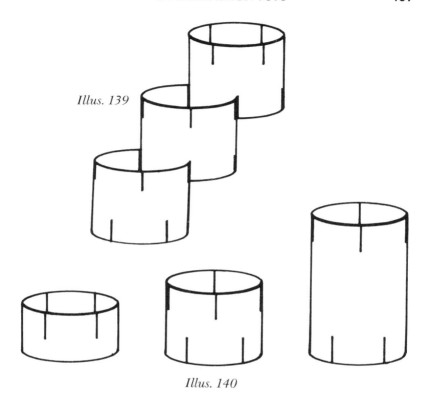

Illus. 139

Illus. 140

The two taller cylinders have the bottom slots offset.

There's no limit as to the different sizes of flat pieces and cylinders you can devise as you expand your set of building pieces. Just take your time and cut out each piece carefully. This paper action toy is good for many building sessions, if you work with care.

5
Moving Action

You've probably made pinwheels before. In this chapter you'll make a folded pinwheel that's different from any pinwheel you've ever made or seen. After you've used your folded pinwheel to make a *Puff and Spin Windmill*, branch out and construct a multiple-pinwheel action toy.

Paper poppers are always fun, especially when they can be folded in just seconds. Target games are great for lots of action. You'll find that using a blowpipe adds to the fun; and *Big Mouth* lets you put words into its mouth.

Puff and Spin Windmill

You've seen pinwheels and played with them. The *Puff and Spin Windmill* you're going to make is a special sort of pinwheel; it doesn't require any cutting.

Begin with a square sheet of notebook paper or other such paper. Once you see how the *Puff and Spin* toy is made, you'll probably want to do some coloring to make it more exciting as it spins. For now, however, we'll use plain white paper, so you can see how to fold this paper action toy. Besides, white blades or sails on a windmill look great.

Begin by folding the paper in half. Crease the fold and unfold it so it looks like Illus. 141. The fold you have in place runs right down the center of the paper.

The two dotted lines in Illus. 141 show exactly where to make your next pair of folds. Fold in both sides, so that their edges meet at the middle fold.

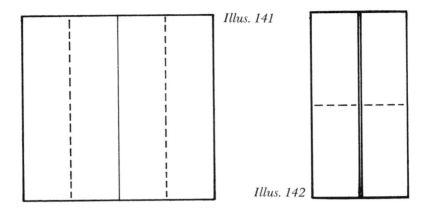

Illus. 141

Illus. 142

Once this bit of folding is finished, *Puff and Spin* is shown in Illus. 142.

The dotted line in Illus. 142 locates your next fold, but don't make it yet. This fold is backwards. Fold the top of the paper *back* along the dotted line. Check Illus. 143 to see how things look after this fold is complete. Now go ahead and make the fold.

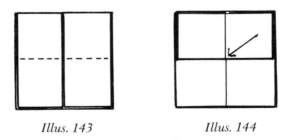

Illus. 143   *Illus. 144*

Your next step is to fold up the top layer of paper along the dotted line shown in Illus. 143.

Once this fold is in place, you've reached Illus. 144.

Here's the tricky part! Check the arrow shown in Illus. 144. Behind the top sheet of paper there are two more layers, which make squares of paper about 2″ on a side. The arrow is pointing to the lower inside corner formed where these two layers of paper meet at a fold.

What you're going to do is to pull out that point of paper and pull to the right, so that it forms the triangular point of paper you see in Illus. 145.

This isn't really difficult, but you do have to be careful not to tear the paper. Just take hold of the corner of paper and turn it inside out. When you finish, crease the paper well. You'll have a triangle of paper behind the top sheet, which is exactly the same size as the triangle sticking out to the right.

Now that you've accomplished this tricky bit of folding, do the same for the left-hand side of the project. Once that fold is turned inside out, your *Puff and Spin* should look like Illus. 146.

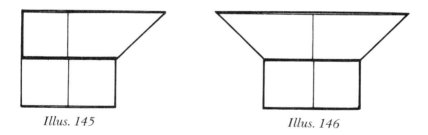

Illus. 145   *Illus. 146*

Turn over the paper from left to right, not upside down. You're now looking at Illus. 147. The dotted line tells you to fold up the bottom of the paper. Once that's done, your *Puff and Spin* is shown in Illus. 148.

It's time to repeat the inside-out business with both corners of the folded paper. When this is done your paper action toy should look just like the one shown in Illus. 149. Both sides match each other.

You know, it really shouldn't be that difficult to pull out that corner.

Unfold the project down the middle, so that it looks like Illus. 150.

The dotted line shows where to fold next. Fold only the top section. Just make the diagonal fold, and you're at Illus. 151.

Make the diagonal fold indicated by the dotted line shown in Illus. 151. But first, check the drawing carefully. This fold goes diagonally across one square section of paper.

Once this fold is in place, your action *Puff and Spin* is shown in Illus. 152.

You now need a strip of cellophane tape or masking tape about 1½″ long. If you don't have tape, a few tiny spots of glue will do, but tape is faster, since it doesn't have to wait to

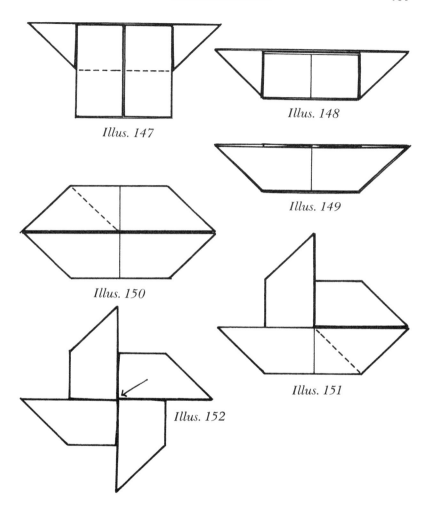

Illus. 147

Illus. 148

Illus. 149

Illus. 150

Illus. 151

Illus. 152

dry. Roll the tape into a little cylinder with the sticky side out. Make sure the ends overlap so that the tape doesn't unroll.

Lift up the top layers of paper at the middle of your project. The arrow in Illus. 152 shows where. Press the little cylinder of tape onto the inside of your *Puff and Spin* pinwheel. Then press the front layers down onto the sticky tape.

This holds everything in place once your action toy is spinning.

Once the tape has the front of the toy stuck to the back, open all four points into little air scoops. The four arrows in Illus. 153 show where you're going to spread the paper to form these air scoops.

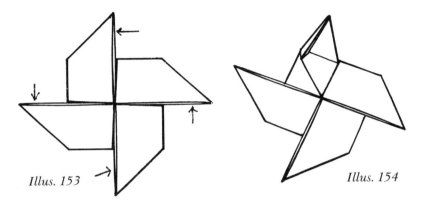

Illus. 153   *Illus. 154*

Illus. 154 shows one air scoop already open and ready for business.

To mount your *Puff and Spin*, just stick a straight pin right through the middle.

For a test spin, push the point of the pin into the eraser on a long pencil or into one end of a plastic drinking straw. Give the toy a spin or two with your hand to make certain that the tape is holding it together in front, and that the air scoops are open.

Illus. 155 shows the pinwheel mounted on a pencil.

To make the toy spin, blow on it from the side so that the air is aimed right at the open scoops. *Puff and Spin* will spin rapidly. If you hold it so the scoops catch the wind, this pinwheel will spin nicely even in a slight breeze.

If you wish, you can play with *Puff and Spin* just like you would any pinwheel. Color or paint it to make it more interesting as it spins away. Let's finish the project and make your *Puff and Spin Windmill.*

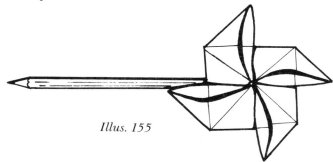

Illus. 155

For the windmill, you need a round box such as one in which breakfast cereals are packaged. A salt container will work but it may be a little small for the sail you just made.

Turn the round cereal box so the open end faces down. This is so you can reach up inside in a few minutes. Either peel off the outer layer of colored paper or wrap the entire box in plain white paper. If you wrap it in white paper, run a few lines of glue up and down the box to hold the paper in place. Or, you can use clear cellophane tape to hold the ends of the paper sheet together. In this case, use a couple of short strips of tape at the bottom of the box to help keep the paper from slipping. Illus. 156 shows the tape in place, if you use tape instead of glue.

Since most round cereal boxes are fairly large, you'll have to use a couple sheets of paper to go around the box.

Now use crayon, paint, or felt-tip markers to add the door and a window or two to your windmill. These additions show up in Illus. 157.

Now to give your windmill a pointed roof. Measure the distance across the top of the carton you're using for your

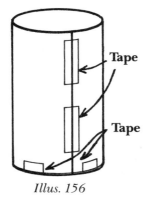

Illus. 156

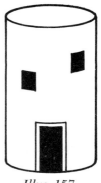

Illus. 157

windmill. You're going to need a half-circle of paper at least twice as far across as the distance across the top of your carton.

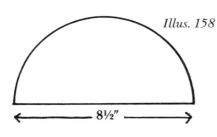

Illus. 158

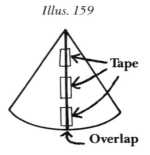

Illus. 159

If your carton is 4″ in diameter, you need to draw a half-circle at least 8″ across. Illus. 158 shows the half-circle already drawn. This half-circle is 8½″ across, which is the width of a piece of typing paper or computer paper.

If you have a compass, that's perfect for drawing half-circles. If not, use a plate or the lid from a cooking pot.

To form the cone, which is the roof for your windmill, grasp the half-circle of paper at the points indicated by the arrows in Illus. 158. Bring these points together and overlap the edges just a bit. Then use a strip or two of tape to hold the cone together. The correctly formed roof is shown in Illus. 159.

Attach the roof to the top of the windmill with three or four little strips of cellophane tape, and you're at Illus. 160.

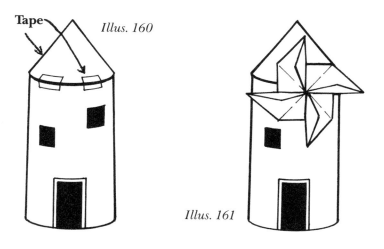

Illus. 160

Illus. 161

To attach the pinwheel (which has become the windmill's sail), just push the straight pin through the side of the carton, and the finished windmill will look much like the one shown in Illus. 161. Set it where a breeze catches the sail, or blow on it to make it spin.

If you have a problem with the pin pulling out or letting the sail tip, cut several small squares of cardboard each about 1″ across. Reach up inside the windmill from the open bottom (if you used a salt container you'll have to cut out the bottom), and carefully press the squares of cardboard onto the sharp end of the pin. Don't stick yourself!

Put a drop of glue on the end of the pin so it doesn't slip back through the pieces of cardboard, and your pinwheel sail should stay firmly in place.

Multiaction Pinwheels

Once you've learned how to fold pinwheels like the one you just used for the windmill, think about making a multiple pinwheel paper action toy.

To begin with, you'll need to fold several pinwheels that are smaller than the one you just made for your windmill. These smaller wheels are a little more difficult to fold because you'll be working with smaller pieces of material, and the air scoops will be harder to form, since there is less working room.

For these reasons, don't be tempted to make your first small pinwheel *too* small. Make your first one from a square of paper that is 6″ on all sides. Then, if you're up to it, make one that begins as a paper square 5″ on a side, and work your way down to smaller squares.

Here's a hint. If you have thinner sheets of paper available, such as lightweight typing or notebook paper, it's easier to fold and shape the smaller pinwheels. Tissue paper or origami paper will enable you to make really small pinwheels.

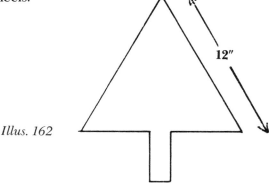

Illus. 162

For your first *Multiaction Pinwheel*, cut out a sheet of cardboard in the shape of a triangle. Make this piece of cardboard about 12″ on all sides, as shown in Illus. 162. Be

Stop! You're cutting the furniture!

extremely careful cutting cardboard. Don't cut yourself, and don't cut tables or other pieces of furniture. Really sharp scissors will cut cardboard without much of a problem.

You can cut out the handle at the same time you do the triangular material, if you wish, so that the entire piece is solid. Or, cut out the handle separately, and glue or tape it securely to the main piece of cardboard.

You're going to mount several pinwheels on this sheet of material, so the finished product should look like Illus. 163. Depending upon the size of the pinwheels you've folded, you may even want to mount an extra one in the middle of the triangle.

Mount the pinwheels with straight pins, just as you did the sail for your windmill. If you have any problem with the pins pulling out, just cut a small square or two of cardboard to go behind the triangular piece of cardboard. Push the pins through these squares just as you did for your windmill. A drop of glue on the end of the pin will hold it in place.

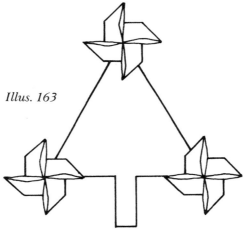

Illus. 163

Remember to leave a bit of space between the back of the pinwheel and the front of the sheet of cardboard. The pinwheel has to have room to turn. If you have a little bead handy, it sometimes helps to slip it onto the pin so it's between the wheel and the mounting board. You can also try to use a tiny circle of cereal-box material, instead of a bead.

Usually you won't have to worry about the wheels not turning, as long as you leave enough room between the wheel and the cardboard.

Now that you see how *Multiaction Pinwheel* is assembled, use color to make this action toy really different. Color the cardboard a light color, such as yellow or light blue or green. Color or paint the pinwheels in bright shades of red, orange, purple, etc.

Some different mounting designs for *Multiaction Pinwheels* are shown in Illus. 164.

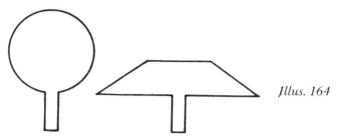

Illus. 164

For variety, think about cutting out the middle of the mounting board. Leave a border about 2″ wide all the way around. Illus. 165 shows how two different mounting shapes look with the middles cut out.

Illus. 165

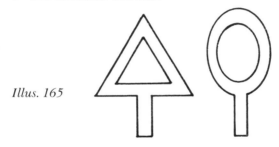

Be very careful when you cut the middles from cardboard pieces. It's easy for you to cut yourself, or a piece of furniture, along with cardboard.

Depending upon the size of your pinwheels, you can mount quite a number of them on one mounting board. Or, you can reduce the size of the mounting board and use only a few small pinwheels.

Remember, in order for these wheels to spin they need to capture the breeze in their air scoops. The mounting board needs to be held at an angle to the wind so that the moving air flows straight into the air scoops.

Quick-Fold Popper

Paper poppers are great fun. This paper action toy is especially fun to use because you can fold it in less than a minute.
All you need is a sheet of notebook paper or typing paper
and you're ready to fold.

Place the paper in front of you, with the long side facing
you. Fold the paper in half and unfold it. The fold gives you
the middle fold seen in Illus. 166. Check the drawing to
make sure you've folded the paper correctly.

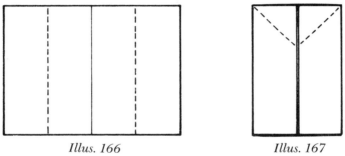

Illus. 166   *Illus. 167*

The two dotted lines in Illus. 166 show where to make your
next folds. Just fold each side in so that the edges meet at the
middle fold.

You've now reached Illus. 167. The two dotted lines in the
drawing indicate your next pair of folds. When you make
these folds, you'll be folding only the top layer of paper.

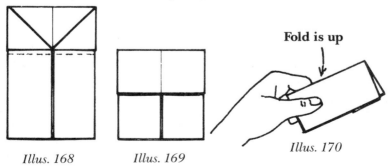

Fold is up

Illus. 168   *Illus. 169*   *Illus. 170*

With this pair of folds in place, your *Quick-Fold Popper* looks like the one shown in Illus. 168.

Fold down the top along the dotted line in Illus. 168. This fold takes you to the drawing in Illus. 169.

Fold over the left side of the popper along the middle fold, which is already in place. Crease this fold carefully. Your *Quick-Fold Popper* is ready for action.

Hold it between your thumb and forefinger, as shown in Illus. 170. Make certain the middle fold is at the top of the popper, or your popper won't pop!

Snap your hand down sharply in order to make the inside of your popper open up with a nice, loud pop. Put a lot of arm motion into this so that your hand and the popper come down hard and fast. That's all there is to it.

Refold the portion of the popper that pops out, and your paper action toy is all set for another pop. If it doesn't pop, just try it again. It may take a few attempts before you find out exactly how much snap you have to give the popper to make it perform properly.

If the popper part tears, just fold a new popper. The *Quick-Fold Popper* only takes a few seconds to make, once you've made your first one.

Blowpipe Target Game

Here's a nifty paper action toy that takes no time at all to make, but it'll give you hours of fun.

A blowpipe is just a sheet of notebook paper or typing paper rolled into a hollow tube. Depending upon which way you roll your sheet of paper, you'll end up with a blowpipe that's either 8½″ long or 11″ long. Either length works just fine, but the longer pipe may give you more accuracy.

Roll the sheet of paper so you end up with a hollow tube that is from ⅝″ to ¾″ across at one end. Before you tape down the loose edge of paper, as seen in Illus. 171, give the tube a bit of a twist, so that one end tightens up. If you look at Illus. 171 you'll notice that one end of the blowpipe is a bit larger than the other. The smaller end needs to be no more than ½" across.

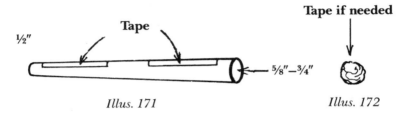

Illus. 171   *Illus. 172*

Once the blowpipe is formed, use a couple of strips of tape to hold the loose edge of the paper in place. These tape strips are shown in Illus. 171.

You're going to hold the smaller end of the blowpipe up to your lips to blow through. The reason for this is safety. Since the mouthpiece end of the blowpipe is smaller than the firing end, you won't accidentally end up with paper-wad ammunition in your mouth.

Now make some ammunition for your target game. Illus. 172 shows a simple paper wad a little more than ½" across. This is the ammunition for your *Blowpipe Target Game*. Crumple a small piece of paper into a tight, round wad. Check to make sure it fits easily into the larger end of your blowpipe. It can't fit so tightly that you can't blow it out; neither can the ammunition wad fit so loosely that lots of air can get around it. If that happens, the wad won't fly out of the blowpipe fast enough to knock over a target.

If you wish, use a bit of tape to secure any loose edges of the paper wad so it doesn't unroll.

Take a few practice puffs to see how much air you have to blow into your blowpipe in order to send the paper wad out properly. Without blowing your brains out, you should be able to fire the ammunition wad 5′ or 6′.

You may find that when you blow into your blowpipe you get a buzzing or honking sound. This little bonus happens because the loose inner edge of the paper vibrates when you blow.

When you blow into your blowpipe, hold the smaller end firmly against your lips with your hand wrapped around it. You don't need to stick the paper tube into your mouth. In fact, if you do, the tube will end up soggy, and you'll have to roll another blowpipe.

You'll want to make several pieces of ammunition so you don't have to shoot your only paper wad over and over. Don't make a career out of wadding small pieces of paper into target ammunition. Make three or four paper wads and get on with the game.

You can fire at anything, such as a food can, and score a point for a hit. If you wish, make a half-dozen targets out of cereal-box material, which will fall over when they're struck.

Cut your first target piece 1½″ wide and 6″ long.

The dotted line in Illus. 173 shows where to fold one end of your target piece. Make this fold about ¾″ from the end of the cardboard.

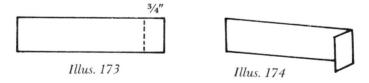

3/4″

Illus. 173   *Illus. 174*

Crease the fold, so that the small end stays at a right angle to the rest of the target. Once you've done this, stand up the target so that it looks like the one shown in Illus. 174.

Set it on the table or the floor or anyplace you're using for your target area and step back a couple of paces. Load your blowpipe, take aim, and blow. If you hit the target and knock it over, you've scored a point.

Make as many targets as you want. Think about making some wider than others, so that they are easier to hit. Knocking over one of these is worth a point. Knocking down a narrow target scores two points. You can even make some targets short and narrow, which are worth three points when knocked down.

This is a great action game for two or more players. Each player has his or her own blowpipe. You can alternate firing and continue until all the targets have been knocked down. If you wish, each player can start with a full group of targets and have three or four shots. Points are scored for all the targets knocked down in the three or four shots. Then the targets are all stood up for the next player's turn.

Big Mouth

This paper action hand puppet lets you put your own words into the puppet's mouth. Watch what you say, because even though *Big Mouth* says the words, *you're* responsible for what it says.

Somewhere you have a small cardboard box that you knew would come in handy someday. Well, that day is today.

Check the cut lines shown in Illus. 175. You're going to make this pair of lines which extend all the way down the side of the little box. Before you cut, be sure that you line up the two cuts so that they're directly across from each other. This is extremely important. Now, go ahead and make these two cuts with your scissors.

If you don't have a small box around, don't worry. You can make one in just seconds from the bottom of a small carton or even from the bottom of a cereal box; just check with Illus. 176.

Be careful where you poke those scissors, will you?

The cut line in the drawing goes all the way around the bottom of the carton. Be careful when you poke the point of your scissors through the side of the carton; then take care that your cut is always the same distance from the bottom.

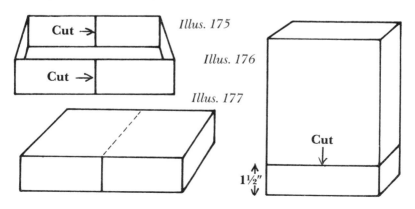

Cut →

Cut →

Illus. 175

Illus. 176

Illus. 177

Cut

1½″

Make this cut about 1½″ up from the bottom, and you'll have a perfect *Big Mouth*.

Once you've cut out the carton bottom, make the side cuts just as you did in Illus. 175.

Turn over the box or carton bottom so that the open side faces downwards. Now fold the left side of the box or carton over along the dotted line shown in Illus. 177.

Now you can see why the cuts have to be directly across from one another; otherwise *Big Mouth* would end up with a crooked mouth.

If you made your cuts exactly halfway between the ends of the box or carton bottom your mouth should be the same both on the top and on the bottom. If the cuts are nearer one end than the other, *Big Mouth* will have one jaw longer than the other. This is just fine. In fact, you may decide you want to make another *Big Mouth* with either its top or bottom jaw longer than the other to give it character.

Slip your thumb into one part of the box and your fingers into the other. Check Illus. 178 to see how this works. If the box is too narrow to hold all your fingers, then let one or more of them stick out to the side.

Illus. 178

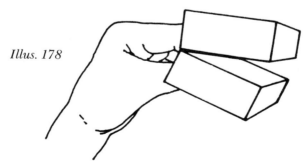

By now you've already discovered that by opening and closing your hand, *Big Mouth* opens and closes.

Decorate *Big Mouth* to suit yourself. Illus. 179 shows a side view of *Big Mouth* showing lots of large teeth. In the same drawing there's a front view, in which *Big Mouth* has a pair of nice, full lips.

Illus. 179

If you used a plain box, just color or use felt-tip markers or paint right on the box. If you cut the bottom from a carton, you'll have several colors and some printing to deal with in order to paint or color *Big Mouth* the way you want it to be.

You can paint over the colors and printing if you have paint available. If you try to cover the markings with felt-tip markers, you'll use up all your marking pens just trying to make the colors dark enough.

What you can do is to wrap plain white paper around the outside of *Big Mouth* and tape or paste the paper onto the box or carton so that the paper stays in place; then color or use felt-tip markers on the paper.

If you wish to give *Big Mouth* a tongue, that's simple. Illus. 180 shows three possible tongue designs. The forked tongue is great if your *Big Mouth* happens to be a dragon.

Illus. 180

Fold or bend the tongue along the dotted line. Run a little bit of glue or paste along the bottom of the narrow folded part. Place this in the hinge of *Big Mouth*'s jaw so its tongue stays in place. Illus. 181 shows a tongue in place.

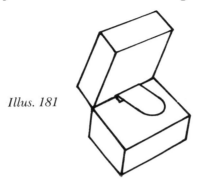

Illus. 181

If you have a *Big Mouth* for each hand, your puppet characters can carry on a conversation. Make several *Big Mouth* characters and write up your own puppet show. Not only is *Big Mouth* a great action toy for you to play with on your own, it's excellent for entertaining others.

6
Solutions

Here are the solutions to *Mental Action* and *Five-Cube Fun*, just in case you need a bit of help.

There are a number of solutions to both puzzle games. Here's one way to solve each. If you've solved them another way, that's wonderful.

Check back to page 16 if you need to review how the moving pieces were numbered for *Mental Action*. With those numbers in mind, here's how to win the game.

1. Jump five over two
2. Jump five over one
3. Jump five over seven
4. Jump five over nine
5. Jump three over six
6. Jump four over eight
7. Jump four over three (which is in nine's space)
8. Jump five over four (which is in six's space)

Piece number five is the only remaining piece, and it's in the middle square. You've just played a winning game.

Here's one of a number of winning solutions for *Five-Cube Fun*.

Begin with the cube numbered with 1's, 2's and 3's only. Place it so the 1 is on top. The 3 should be facing you.

Now locate the cube numbered 1, 2, 3, 4, 4, 5. Place it on top of the first cube so that the 5 is on top. The two should be facing you.

Your next cube is the one numbered 1, 1, 3, 4, 4, 5. Set it on top of the other two cubes with the five on top. Turn it so that a 1 faces you and a four is facing to your left. This means there will be a 1 facing to your right.

The fourth cube is numbered 1, 1, 3, 4, 5, 5. Set it on the other cubes so you have a 1 on top and a 4 on the bottom. Turn the cube so that there is a 5 facing you and a 3 to your left. There will be a 5 to your right.

The final cube is numbered, 2, 2, 3, 4, 5, 5. Place it on the top of the stack with 2 facing up and 2 facing down. The 4 must face you so it has a 5 on its left and a 3 to the right.

Now check each of the four numbered stacks. All four sides of the stack of cubes will contain the numbers 1, 2, 3, 4, and 5. The numbers are not in order, but all five numbers are on all sides of the stack. Once again, you're a winner.

Metric Equivalents

INCHES TO MILLIMETRES AND CENTIMETRES

MM—millimetres   *CM—centimetres*

Inches	MM	CM	Inches	CM	Inches	CM
⅛	3	0.3	9	22.9	30	76.2
¼	6	0.6	10	25.4	31	78.7
⅜	10	1.0	11	27.9	32	81.3
½	13	1.3	12	30.5	33	83.8
⅝	16	1.6	13	33.0	34	86.4
¾	19	1.9	14	35.6	35	88.9
⅞	22	2.2	15	38.1	36	91.4
1	25	2.5	16	40.6	37	94.0
1¼	32	3.2	17	43.2	38	96.5
1½	38	3.8	18	45.7	39	99.1
1¾	44	4.4	19	48.3	40	101.6
2	51	5.1	20	50.8	41	104.1
2½	64	6.4	21	53.3	42	106.7
3	76	7.6	22	55.9	43	109.2
3½	89	8.9	23	58.4	44	111.8
4	102	10.2	24	61.0	45	114.3
4½	114	11.4	25	63.5	46	116.8
5	127	12.7	26	66.0	47	119.4
6	152	15.2	27	68.6	48	121.9
7	178	17.8	28	71.1	49	124.5
8	203	20.3	29	73.7	50	127.0

Index